INTERNATIONAL ECONOMIC INTEGRATION

INTERNATIONAL ECONOMIC INTEGRATION
SECOND, REVISED, EDITION

BY

JAN TINBERGEN

Professor of Development Planning,
Netherlands School of Economics, Rotterdam

ELSEVIER PUBLISHING COMPANY
AMSTERDAM-LONDON-NEW YORK
1965

ELSEVIER PUBLISHING COMPANY
335 JAN VAN GALENSTRAAT, P.O. BOX 211, AMSTERDAM

AMERICAN ELSEVIER PUBLISHING COMPANY, INC.
52 VANDERBILT AVENUE, NEW YORK, N.Y. 10017

ELSEVIER PUBLISHING COMPANY LIMITED
12B, RIPPLESIDE COMMERCIAL ESTATE
RIPPLE ROAD, BARKING, ESSEX

LIBRARY OF CONGRESS CATALOG CARD NUMBER 64-15301

WITH 12 ILLUSTRATIONS AND 8 TABLES

PREFACE TO FIRST EDITION

This book, in a way, constitutes a second edition of my «International Economic Co-operation» (published in 1945), which has been completely re-written in order to take into account the rapid development in thinking as well as in international economic co-operation itself. As the change in title indicates, the emphasis has also been slightly shifted: the process of integration has been chosen as the aim towards which the analysis is directed.

The booklet is meant, as in its first edition, for those not officially trained or not yet trained in economics and tries to stick to simple language. Nevertheless it tries to concentrate on the economic background of the integration process rather than on events or documentation; economic reasoning is its main instrument. In two appendices the foundations of this reasoning are illustrated in some more detail

1954   J.T.

PREFACE TO SECOND EDITION

This new edition has been adapted to the rapid changes in economic facts and the progress made in international economic integration, both in Europe and elsewhere.

My sincere thanks are due to Mr. M. Kristein, who revised the idiom.

1964   J.T.

V

CONTENTS

SUMMARY OF CONTENTS

PART I – THE ESSENCE OF INTERNATIONAL ECONOMIC RELATIONS BETWEEN AUTONOMOUS NATIONS

1 – *Introduction; the Heterogeneity of World Economy*

1.1 – This book is written for the general public interested in problems of international economic co-operation, not for specialists. Its two Parts try to give, respectively, an insight into the nature of international economic relations in a world of autonomous governments, and into the question: in what respect should these relations be deliberately regulated in an «integrated» world.

1.2 – The world economy consists of a great number of national economies. In some respects these are almost watertight compartments, but in other respects they are closely connected. There is a considerable difference in *population* and in *wealth* between the national economies. This wealth consists of natural resources and capital goods; some figures are quoted.

1.3 – Areas of different structure distinguished by Kirschen.

1.4 – In each of the national economies goods and services are produced with the help of the three so-called *factors of production:* nature or land, labour and capital.

1.5 – *Production per head* depends on the quantities of land and of capital available per head, on the education of the population and on the institutional framework within which production is organized.

1.6 – Hence the great differences in *prosperity*. China and India are the principal underdeveloped areas of the world. The total product is divided among the factors labour, land and capital in proportions which, curiously enough, do not vary greatly for different countries; broadly speaking they are 70, 10 and 20 per cent.

1.7 – There are the following possibilities of economic intercourse between nations:

[1] Transfer of *products:* mainly against other products in the form of current trade; incidentally in the form of gifts or other unilateral transfers;

[2] Transfer of *factors of production:* [a] persons: migration; [b] land: change of territory; [c] capital: capital imports and exports.

Transfer [2b] is not frequent; it may occur as a consequence of political events. In the interwar period [2a] did not occur frequently either. By far the most important forms of intercourse are, therefore, [1] and [2c].

2 – *Current Transactions*

2.1 – Current transactions between countries are those in products, i.e. goods and services, excluding those in factors of production. Each country will export products which it is able to produce at lower cost than other countries. Low-price products are not likely to move over long distances. Large countries are likely to have a smaller percentage of foreign trade than small countries.

2.2 – Generally, transactions will be *multilateral.* A distinction is made between [i] net surplus or deficit for any country, [ii] bilateral, [iii] circular and [iv] open flow component. In a situation of equilibrium [i] does not exist; for the world at large [iv] cannot exist. The structure of commercial transactions between four broad subdivisions of the world is given: surpluses and deficits.

2.3 – Trade may be [i] *free,* [ii] *hampered* more or less arbitrarily or [iii] *controlled.* Trade may be hampered by quantitative restrictions, currency restrictions or import duties. There may be blocks of countries with [i] free trade internally and [ii] a common tariff for the outside world [*customs unions*] or without such a common tariff [*free trade areas*]. We speak of *integration* or an economic union if other aspects of economic policy also are unified so as to present an optimum of centralization.

2.4 – With *free trade,* prices of international goods are – apart from transportation costs – uniform throughout the world; and trade will be multilateral. Even with free trade there may be *imperfect competition,* e.g. because of distances. The short-term elasticity of the share of any one country in world trade with respect to its relative price level appears to be no more than 2. The short-term elasticity of import quotas appears also to be rather low. Probably, long-term elasticities are higher.

2.5 – International trade as a consequence of differences between countries in relative efficiency in producing various commodities [*theory of comparative cost*]. Differences in standard of living as a consequence of differences in efficiency in producing all or most commodities.

2.6 – *The fundamental thesis of the doctrine of free trade:* With full employment of all resources and marginal cost pricing, free trade yields – in the long run – a maximum of total production and hence, apart from certain questions of distribution, a maximum of welfare. Every deviation from it therefore means, for small countries, a smaller prosperity; it can only be an advantage for some groups within those countries at the expense of other groups in the same countries. Large countries may, by tariff policy, improve their terms of trade and their real expenditure. Marginal cost pricing may not be possible in certain industries without subsidization. Subsidies are to be preferred to protection. Without full employment being guaranteed beforehand, protection may, in some country, cause an increase in employment and therefore raise prosperity. The maintenance of full employment requires a compensatory financial policy.

2.7 – Protection may help to break the shock of a *sudden adaptation* to new circumstances or to stimulate infant industries. The danger of protection is in the possible persistence of less productive units.

2.8 – Generally, liberalization of trade will also mean the disruption of bilateral equilibria. Therefore, it can only be attained if at the same time a certain convertibility of currencies is re-established.

2.9 – Customs unions may, but need not, be a step towards world free trade: «*trade diversion*» versus «*trade creation*» [Viner].

3 – *International Movements of Factors: Land, Labour and Capital*

3.1 – Movements of *land* in the literal sense are, of course, impossible. The transfer of territory from one nation to another may, however, be considered as an example. So far, such a transfer has not been considered a possible element of economic policy.

3.2 – Movements of labour, i.e. of *population,* or migration have been important

X

for the areas of immigration, such as the United States of America, but, as a rule, only of minor significance to the areas of emigration. Since 1914 the extent of migratory movements has been very restricted. It is to be hoped that, under certain guarantees, the less populated countries will be prepared to revise their policies.

3.3 – From the economic point of view, *capital* movements represent by far the most important form of international movements of factors of production. These may take the form of loans in the narrower sense or of participation; loans [in the wider sense, i.e. including participation] come down, in real terms, to the transfer of commodity stocks [durable and non-durable goods] from the lending to the borrowing area at the price of an annual «mortgage» on part of the latter's production. Usually, the lending area will be one of the highly developed countries and the borrowing area one of the underdeveloped countries, where the marginal productivity of capital will be higher. In this way a decrease in the inequality in living conditions may be obtained. So far, however, the divergence in living conditions between developed and underdeveloped countries has increased. Obstacles to capital movements are to be found in uncertain political conditions, unstable financial and monetary conditions, or low efficiency of production. The vicious circle of low productivity due to the lack of external economies and low capital formation; the possibility of its being broken by an international investment policy.

3.4 – Short-term capital movements are of much less direct significance for the trend of development but may contribute to the maintenance of financial stability and, hence, contribute indirectly to development.

4 – *The Mechanism of Financial Transactions*

4.1 – Only *gold* is accepted everywhere as a means of payment. As payment in gold involves high costs, other means of payment have developed – paper money – the value of which is based on law and confidence and is therefore restricted to a certain area. Payment to foreign countries thus requires a «*transfer*», i.e. a transformation of home into foreign currency. This is effectuated by exchanging the various currencies against each other at a certain market price [the *rate of exchange*]. Sometimes there is more than one market [*multiple exchange rates*].

4.2 – The set of all payments made in a certain period between a country and all other countries is called its *balance of payments*. It may be subdivided into the *current items* [balance of trade, or imports and exports of goods; and invisible imports and exports or payments for services: shipping, interest, tourism etc.] and the *capital items* [import and export of capital: long-term and short-term; and the balancing item of gold shipments]. In addition, *unilateral payments* may occur in the balance of payments, e.g. foreign aid and reparation payments.

4.3 – If the equilibrating item is included, there is always equilibrium [*formal* equilibrium]; if it is not included, the phrase «the balance of payments» has a different meaning. It may or may not be in equilibrium [*material* equilibrium]. In the long run there must be material equilibrium; otherwise there would be a permanent accumulation of gold somewhere and a permanent drain elsewhere. A modest drain may, however, be almost a permanent phenomenon. Long-run material equilibrium must also exist, for similar reasons, for any part of a currency area.

4.4 – *Stability of exchange rates* is an advantage for economic calculations, but it may be non-compatible with stable prices, which are desirable for other reasons. Usually, fixed rates, with incidental revisions, are preferred. With the «*gold standard*», there is a fixed price in each country against which the Central Bank buys or sells gold. The corresponding rate of exchange is called the *parity rate*. On both sides of parity there are rates called the «*gold points*», indicating the limits within which gold shipments are unremunerative. Only a rigorous material equilibrium in the balance of payments will maintain the exchange rates between the gold points. If one of the gold points is reached, a movement of gold will follow, tending to keep the rate of exchange at that point. If it should go on for some time there is the threat of an exhaustion of the gold stock of one of the countries concerned. This can be prevented by [a] «indirect» or [b] «direct» action.

4.5 – Indirect action may be [1] automatic, resulting from the changes in the monetary circulation: a decrease in gold stock leading to a decrease in note circulation or deposits, a reduction in incomes and hence reduced imports and lower prices which will stimulate exports. This automatism does not, however, work very strongly and quickly. Indirect action may also be [2] deliberate interference, i.e. *raising the rate of discount* in the threatened [deficit] country. This leads partly to the same results [though again only weakly and slowly], and partly to more important changes, namely an influx of short-term credits from abroad – provided there are no counteracting factors such as lack of confidence. This remedy can, however, only work temporarily: after some time a new equilibrium in the capital market will be reached. The «defence of the Dutch guilder» during 1935/6.

4.6 – Direct action is equivalent to *stopping the sale of gold;* this means either the end of the free gold standard or of the previous parity. The old parity may be maintained at the cost of freedom. Of course, the danger of an exhaustion of the gold stock is smallest when a country has a large gold reserve.

4.7 – Apart from gold, a country's currency system may be based upon [1] other currencies [gold exchange standard] or [2] other commodities [silver, raw materials]. Consequences of a *raw material standard:* stabilization of the average price level of raw materials and reduction of cyclic movements as far as they are due to «accounting errors» in income determination.

4.8 – In principle, the system of *flexible rates* operates in the same way as the gold standard. The chosen limits between which the rate of exchange is allowed to fluctuate can be wider or narrower. Smaller fluctuations may be counteracted by the operations of an *equalization fund.* In the longer run, changes in the rate of exchange will be helpful to equilibrate the balance of payments, since they affect imports and exports via the price system. By permitting only gradual movements, the influence of speculation may be kept down, which has proved disastrous in a number of cases [Germany 1923].

5 – Disequilibrium and Equilibrium in the Balance of Payments

5.1 – In this chapter some consequences of disequilibrium will be considered; the conditions for equilibrium will be formulated and some techniques of short-term adaptation discussed. With multilateral equilibrium, i.e. equilibrium in the balances of payments of all countries, there will be the possibility of *complete convertibility*.

5.2 – If not every balance of payments is in equilibrium there will be deficit and surplus countries. The currency reserves of the deficit countries will gradually diminish. Once reserves are exhausted the currency of a country will be inconvertible or a «*soft currency*» as distinguished from «*hard*» *currencies*. The «degree of softness».

5.3 – *Partial convertibility* may be instituted by decree, but can be maintained only if the country concerned is near to the equilibrium position which is relevant to the type of convertibility considered. It may refer to convertibility into some other currency or to certain types of transactions. Convertibility with respect to current transactions with a given group of other countries requires that the total of these transactions – under the new circumstances – be in equilibrium. The «new circumstances» imply the shifts in transactions as a consequence of convertibility itself.

5.4 – Detailed examination of consequences.

5.5 – Convertibility for all transactions, including *capital transactions,* is exposed to far greater risks, because of the incalculability of switches in capital assets that the public may desire. Example of the British convertibility attempt in 1947. Convertibility of currency A into currency B and of B into C has to imply convertibility of A into C also; there have to be groups of mutually convertible currencies, consisting of currencies of about equal strength.

5.6 – Equivalence, for small countries, of *balance of payments equilibrium* and *spending equilibrium;* inflationary and deflationary gap. Meaning of monetary equilibrium for small and for large countries. Regulation of national expenditure and of the price level is needed in order to maintain balance of payments equilibrium at a level of high and stable employment. Multiple exchange rates as a second-best in the absence of other means.

5.7 – Equilibrium, as just described, to be understood as one *relative to other countries*. Possibility of world inflation. «*Imported*» inflation and «*exported*» inflation.

5.8 – In order to attain or to maintain equilibrium in the balances of payments various instruments are available. A distinction may be made between:

[1] autonomous *changes in quantities demanded,* without changes in price ratios or absolute prices; and

5.9 – [2] *changes in price ratios,* inducing changes in quantities, and themselves to be obtained by: [i] direct changes in absolute prices; [ii] indirect changes, i.e. changes in wage levels or rates of exchange.

A closer examination reveals that:

[A] sometimes price ratios need not be changed, if the automatic quantitative reactions to the disturbing forces already restore equilibrium; and

5.10 – [B] in other cases price ratio changes do not work (the case of the *critical* or nearly critical *elasticities* of imports and exports); [C] in still other cases price changes do work, but cannot be obtained by changes in wage or exchange rates [the case of purely static reactions]; [D] and hence price ratio changes, when necessary, can be obtained by wage or exchange rate policy only under certain conditions. In case B, autonomous changes in quantities demanded [such as an «austerity policy» or continued imports of capital or the cancellation of debts] are the only solution; in case C either direct price policy or autonomous changes in quantities will be necessary.

PART II – INTERNATIONAL ECONOMIC INTEGRATION

6 – Targets and Instruments of International Economic Integration

6.1 – After having dealt with the nature of international economic relations between autonomous nations and the possibilities of regulating them, we shall now discuss how far we want to regulate them, or in modern terms, how far we want to *integrate* the various national economies. This problem of integration has to be seen as a part of the more general problem of the *optimum economic policy*. When making recommendations of economic policy we are to some extent leaving the territory of economic science. We shall be careful to warn the reader each time we do so.

6.2 – It is useful, in order to clarify problems of economic policy, to distinguish between *qualitative* and *quantitative* policy. Qualitative policy is a change in organization; quantitative policy is a change, within a given type of organization, of certain data to be called *instruments*. Changes in organization may be of a very fundamental character and then be called reforms or even revolutions; or they may be changes in details of organization. Quantitative policies may use either a large or a small number of instruments, and a distinction may be made between direct and indirect policies, in that the former directly interfere with market forces and the latter only indirectly.

6.3 – An important aspect of qualitative changes in policy is the one of *centralization* or *decentralization*, especially in international affairs.

6.4 – Directives for the desirable degree of centralization in international economic policy: decentralization of *neutral*, or almost neutral, instruments and centralization of clearly *supporting* and clearly *conflicting* instruments.

6.5 – The choice of a policy has to depend on circumstances and will, in addition, be a question of taste. Necessity of a policy of intervention in cases of serious disturbances or of serious emergencies. Differences in tastes and pre-conceived ideas also determine the choice of instruments. Examples are quoted.

6.6 – The *aims* of economic policy cannot be formulated on the basis of economic science alone. Welfare is dependent on individual well-being and the relations with other individuals. Incomparability of satisfaction of different individuals and the resulting difficulties. Almost generally accepted aims are those of *high production* and a *more equal distribution* in cases of marked inequality. High production requires the *use of all productive resources* [implying avoidance of instability] and the use of these resources in the *most efficient* way. The use of instruments of detailed intervention should be restricted to the *prevention of strong disequilibria*.

6.7 – The differences in economic policy between the communist and the noncommunist countries may partly be explained by factors that are strong enough to make it impossible to aim at one world policy. International relations with communist countries have to be highly centralized. Only relations between noncommunist countries may be adapted to what we consider an optimum degree of centralization.

6.8 – Problem of integration to be dealt with, firstly, in terms of national instruments and, secondly, in terms of international instruments of economic policy.

7 – *Minimum Conditions for Integration*

7.1 – Economic integration may assume weaker or stronger forms, depending on the degree of centralization of the alternative instruments. Weak forms of centralization are those of consultation, stronger forms are those of co-ordination, with the strongest form being complete unification.

7.2 – In the latter case the integrated area will have one central government dealing with those instruments requiring centralized handling, and lower public authorities will supervise the other instruments. Many institutions and instruments will show uniform features although such uniformity is not necessary for the proper operation of an area's economy.

7.3 – However, a number of institutions and instruments need not be uniform, or even co-ordinated. Generally speaking, instruments of an almost neutral character can be left in the hands of lower authorities and need not be co-ordinated. This applies to regulating markets of a local character, to taxes affecting such markets, and to some extent even to direct taxes generally.

7.4 – Countries desiring integration must, however, satisfy certain conditions with regard to their non-neutral instruments of economic policy. In the terminology introduced previously they should adapt their use of supporting and conflicting instruments to the international requirements. Perhaps the most important condition is that they should maintain *spending equilibrium at a high level of employment*.

7.5 – There are two main groups of instruments for this policy and a number of subsidiary ones. The first main group is that of *financial policy,* consisting of public expenditure policy and tax policy. By an appropriate manipulation of these instruments, total internal demand will be kept at the desired level and its composition may be made optimum.

7.6 – The second group of instruments is that of *wages or exchange rates*. Either of them may be used to adjust the general price level of the country to its competitive strength and, hence, to regulate foreign demand.

7.7 – Necessity of understanding in business circles for the measures just discussed.

7.8 – Desirability of a centralized use of the instruments of economic policy is discussed. In view of the strong resistance to integration in this field, the centralization might be confined to central decisions about the «inflationary» or «deflationary» gap in the public sector and the general price level of each country.

7.9 – These two main groups of instruments may have to be supplemented by others, in order to make minor adjustments. *Temporary subsidies, specific taxes* or even *temporary import duties* may be necessary to support industries or regions whose competitive power falls short of the requirements. In the case of sudden disturbances of equilibrium or of particular industries, *quantitative* regulations may be needed. None of these policies should, in the long run, hamper the correct use of the productive resources from the international point of view.

8 – *The Integration of Current Transactions*

8.1 – In this chapter the use of the *non-monetary instruments* of economic policy in an integrated area will be discussed wherever pertinent to the integration of current transactions. A distinction will be made between *negative* and *positive integration,* but first the reader will be reminded of some *recent developments* in integration policies in Europe, Latin America, the Arab region, Central Africa and South-East Asia.

8.2 – *Negative integration,* being the abolition of instruments harmful to the common well-being of the integrated area, is required above all else in trade impediments. Both quantitative restrictions and import duties should be eliminated but a *gradual* abolition recommends itself as an optimum in order to reduce transition losses.

8.3 – Certain well-known *exceptions* (agriculture, energy, infant industries) may be admitted. *Subsidies are preferable,* however, in so far as organizational difficulties are not too large.

8.4 – Abolition of duties will require adjustments in the *rates of exchange.*

8.5 – *Positive integration* requires, as a minimum, co-ordinating the use of some instruments in order to avoid a falsification of the price formation and the ensuing division of labour. Requirements for *indirect* taxes are formulated.

8.6 – In a modern mixed economy, integration also implies the organization at the community level of the institutions and means required for the maximum of welfare.

8.7 – *Redistribution of incomes* and the *regulation of unstable markets,* especially in agriculture, are examples; so is *planning.* Subsidies for regional development must not falsify price formation in the transportation sector.

8.8 – An attempt is made to estimate the *extent* of the *consequences* of integration.

9 – *Monetary Integration*

9.1 – This chapter deals with the *monetary* instruments, i.e. with the techniques of international payments and their integration. The simplest theoretical solution would be the introduction of a *world currency,* but political unity would be its prerequisite. It is probable, moreover, that the flight of capital from war-threatened countries would disturb such a monetary system. It is impossible to liberalize capital transactions completely.

9.2 – A system of national currencies almost equivalent to a world currency. A policy of *flexible exchange rates,* as advocated before World War II, seemed useful during the confusion of the Great Depression, but implies more arbitrariness than seems desirable. Something more similar to the gold standard, with a *minimum of autonomous changes,* seems more attractive. Disadvantages of the use of key currencies for reserve purposes; desirability to create *international reserve assets.*

9.3 – The changes should be under international control, but in practice this is difficult. Their frequency will be reduced if equilibrium in the balances of payments is preserved as much as possible. National *reserves* and an *international equalization fund,* such as the I.M.F., will be helpful to overcome short-term disequilibria. In order to warrant long-term equilibrium, national policies should be directed towards *spending equilibrium* and a *competitive price and wage level.*

9.4 – Apart from these policies, *capital movements* may help to maintain equilibrium. Short-term capital movements are not always helpful [«hot money»], and long-term movements might be used for this purpose to a greater extent. The distribution of a country's assets and liabilities over the various degrees of liquidity should be such as not to disturb equilibrium.

9.5 – Some of the most important *disequilibria* between currencies created by the *Second World War* have gradually been overcome. Western European currencies have regained strength, especially those of the European Economic Community. Dollar strength has been replaced by some weakness in the dollar position. Many developing countries remain in a difficult situation.

9.6 – *Monetary integration* of the non-communist world may be strengthened further by [i] *increased* capital and income *transfers* to developing countries, [ii] a more systematic procedure to create international liquidities to the extent needed and [iii] a *better financial structure* in many developing countries.

10 – *The Integration of Development*

10.1 – So far, international economic policy has been discussed on the basis of a given distribution of resources over nations. As was indicated already in Chapter 1, this distribution, however, is far from satisfactory. Its extreme unevenness may be a source of important future tensions: the *divergency of living standards* threatens political unity.

10.2 – *Factor price equalization* only works to a limited extent as long as factors are not permitted to move. Necessity for factors to move, i.e. of capital transfers and population transfers. Necessity, also, of integrating the process of growth. Impossibility of neglecting *population problem*.

10.3 – Raising the standards of life of the poorer countries by decree is an economic impossibility: prescription of higher wages, e.g., will lead to more unemployment. Rise in *production* needed, requiring a simultaneous increase in *capital* and *training* and spread of *technical knowledge*. Nature of investments needed first. Impossibility of increasing capital formation inside the countries concerned to a sufficient degree.

10.4 – *Order of magnitude* of capital transfers needed in order to stop divergency of living standards. Order of magnitude of present capital transfers. Impossibility of attracting private capital from abroad. Desirability of an «*international budget*». Necessity of an efficient use of capitals and manpower involved.

10.5 – An efficient use of capital and manpower requires the establishment of national and international *development plans*. In many countries such plans now exist or are in preparation. Their mutual consistency as well as the efficiency of their construction will be enhanced by an *international development plan*. Preparations for such a plan are being made. Integrating the development of the developing continents requires an intimate co-operation between governments, especially for the creation of heavy industry.

10.6 – In the future division of labour between developed and less developed countries the former must concentrate on industries requiring a relatively large amount of research and having a large optimum size, leaving the labour-intensive industries and those with a small optimum size to the developing countries.

11 – *The Agencies of International Economic Co-operation*

11.1 – The preceding chapters have described a system of international economic policy and the corresponding tasks in various fields. We will now discuss what *agencies* will have to be charged with these tasks. To what extent will the existing national agencies be able to perform them, to what extent will they have to be switched over to existing or new international agencies? These problems are intimately connected with the problem of *political integration*. The common economic policy itself may be more or less interventionist which should also depend on circumstances. As long as the preparedness to co-operate falls short of the degree of co-operation needed, less effective methods will have to be followed. Tasks of local or national interest only should, of course, be left to local or national organs. It is primarily where one government may adversely or favourably affect the interests of other nations that a *central agency* will be needed. In the former case, the central agency will be a supervising rather than an active agency. Agencies to be arranged according to *instruments* of economic policy. General and partial instruments and agencies. From our survey it has become clear that *general* agencies will be needed for six groups of tasks, to be discussed in succession. In principle, all these tasks should be performed on a world-wide basis. Given the unhappy controversy between the communist and the non-communist countries, incomplete provisions may be unavoidable. Moreover, *regional integration* may be useful as an example or because of differences in technical level. In principle, agencies have been created by the United Nations for each of the six main tasks indicated, but various difficulties have been encountered.

11.2 – *The supervision and reduction of trade restrictions* should have been the task of the ITO, which has not, however, come into existence. Although the tasks with regard to trade restrictions have been taken over by the GATT, progress has been slow as a consequence of the opposition of vested interests and the complicated techniques used in tariff negotiations. Considerable progress has been made within the *European Economic Community* and prospects for success over a wider area have been opened up by the authorization recently given to the American government to negotiate linear reductions in tariffs. Problems surrounding the Common Market and the Cotton Textiles Agreement.

11.3 – *The regulation of raw material markets* is entrusted, in principle, to the FAO and the Committee for International Commodity Trade of the United Nations. Wheat, sugar, tin, coffee and tea international agreements are in operation, but efforts to secure agreements on other commodities have not been successful so far. Although recent prospects have improved, it may be felt that a more effective means is available in the *insurance scheme* against export declines proposed by the United Nations Secretariat.

11.4 – *The supervision of the convertibility of currencies* and a number of related tasks are entrusted to the *International Monetary Fund*. Since the Fund's means can only be used for the compensation of temporary deficits, it cannot solve the long-term problems facing many developing countries. The Fund's structure raises two fundamental questions: [a] is it desirable for many countries to use *key currencies* as their reserve material and [b] how can *world liquidity* be regulated most effectively? Professor Triffin's proposals.

11.5 – *The supervision of monetary equilibrium and employment policies* is less clearly the task of an existing agency. The most effective forms of co-ordination so far applied in this field are those of the periodic «*examinations*» within the OEEC and OECD and the consultations in the *Monetary Committee* of the EEC At the world level the *annual discussion in Ecosoc* plays a similar role, but all these represent a very weak form of co-ordination. Application of the OEEC method would represent a step forward, but more effective forms of co-ordination are highly desirable.

11.6 – *The task of supplying capital to developing countries* is carried out by various agencies with different degrees of centralization. Some developed countries have *bilateral* programs, while some groups of countries have more general schemes [Colombo Plan, EEC, Alliance for Progress]. At the highest international level the U.N. *Special Fund,* the *International Bank for Reconstruction and Development,* the *International Finance Corporation* and the *International Development Association* [the latter two administered by the Bank] are increasingly active.

11.7 – Part of the tasks described under 11.3. [the Insurance Scheme], 11.5 and 11.6 might be entrusted to an *International Treasury,* handling an ordinary budget of current expenditure and thereby able effectively to direct the financial policies of the international community.

11.8 – The *transfer of knowledge* and *education assistance* are tasks performed by various members of the United Nations family of institutions, including FAO and UNESCO.

11.9 – Summary of findings; centres of activity from which fresh initiatives may emanate; the desirability of financial integration is the most important single conclusion reached.

TABLES

DIAGRAMS

MAP

PART I – THE ESSENCE OF INTERNATIONAL ECONOMIC RELATIONS BETWEEN AUTONOMOUS NATIONS

I - INTRODUCTION; THE HETEROGENEITY OF WORLD ECONOMY

1.1 – This book is an attempt to clarify the main problems of international economics and of international economic policy for those who are not economists by profession, but who take an interest in these problems. Not being written for specialists, it tries to give a simple approach to the problems without neglecting, however, some of the complications that have proved to be of importance for dealing with the problems of international economic co-operation. For the same reason it also deals with some common misunderstandings about the subject.

The *desirability of international co-operation* is taken as the starting point of this book. International co-operation is conceivable in nearly every field of human activity. Economic co-operation is only one of its aspects. It has sometimes been considered as the basic aspect, particularly by those who consider economic relations to be generally basic to human relations. The big and dramatic interruptions of international co-operation which we call wars have, in this same train of thought, been explained by economic causes. The occurrence of the Second World War has shown the limits of this philosophy only too clearly. Certainly, autonomous factors of another kind are at work in the causation of war and hence other forms of co-operation than purely economic co-operation will be very important in the struggle for peace. Nevertheless, economic factors remain of importance too, by the simple fact that economic activity must necessarily, in a poor world, take up a large part of total human life. International economic co-operation, therefore, still constitutes an essential part of international co-operation generally. This text deals with its nature and problems. In Part I we will consider the essence of international relations in the economic field. Part II is devoted to the question: in what respect should these relations be the subject of deliberate regulation? In a modern terminology, we deal with international economic *integration* taking this term to mean the optimum of international economic co-operation.

3

1.2 – International economic relations is a subject by itself because of the fact that the *world economy is not homogeneous*. On the contrary, the world is divided into more than a hundred national economies which show wide differences in their more relevant features and are themselves often not very homogeneous. In several respects these national economies are almost independent from each other; in other respects, however, they are intimately connected, as will become clear from our further analysis.

In order to get a first, rough picture of the heterogeneity of the world economy we may describe the national economies by taking their *population* and their *wealth*. It is well known that populations show large differences in quantity as well as in quality. The wealth of any nation consists of two components: [i] its *natural wealth,* such as land for agricultural purposes, minerals, natural means of communication, geographic position and climate, and [ii] the *capital goods* it owns, i.e. the goods partly produced by human labour which are used for further production or consumption: buildings, roads, harbours, machinery, raw material stocks, stocks of consumer goods. Table 1.2 gives some figures about the population and the wealth per head of some of the most important national economies.

Apart from differences in physical wealth, there are differences in *abilities* of the population, in *market* and *social organization* and in *social climate* which may account for the differences in output per head. A big and uniform market, for example, enables a population to apply large-scale methods of production which cannot be used in small areas. Free competition may be a better stimulus to production than rather rigid forms of social organization. Countries with good «industrial relations», i.e. good relations between management and employees, may show better productivity figures, etc. Very little is as yet known about the exact influence of each of these factors on the level of productivity.

1.3 – A modern attempt at a subdivision of the world into more homogeneous regions has been undertaken by Professor E. S. Kirschen[1] from whose study the following table has been derived, which is self-explanatory. (See table 1.3.)

1. E. S. KIRSCHEN, « *Vers un modèle prévisionnel mégisto-économique*», Cahiers Economiques de Bruxelles, 1962, No. 16, p. 471.

TABLE 1.2

Population, Area per Head and Capital per Head for some Countries before World War II[1]

Countries	Population on 31 Dec. 1938 in millions	Area in km² per 1000 inhabitants[2]	Capital in I.U.[3] per head of the working population[4]
U.S.A.	131	61	4360
Canada	11	870	4240
Gt. Britain and N. Ireland	48	5.1	5000
France	42	13.1	2740
Netherlands	9	4.0	2910
Germany and Austria	76	7.5	2670
Italy	44	7.3	1460
Poland	35	11.3	1200
Australia	7	1130	4400
Russia	170	124	1130
Japan	73	5.5	1350
India and Pakistan	395	12.8	580
China	500	133	180

1. No more recent figures about capital are given in COLIN CLARK, *The Conditions of Economic Progress*, 2nd ed., London, 1951.
2. AROUND 1936; *Statistisches Jahrbuch für das Deutsche Reich*, 1937, p. 7.
3. Dollars with the purchasing power of 1925–1934.
4. COLIN CLARK, *The Economics of 1960*, p. 80.

1.4 – In each of the national economies there is a complex *process of production* going on: goods and services are being created with the aid of the three so-called factors of production: labour, nature or land and capital. These three factors are the same elements which we have already discussed. Labour is supplied by the population and the main natural forces are those of climate and soil. As is well known, very different goods and services are being produced: agricultural products such as wheat, rice, potatoes, cotton, butter, etc.; mineral raw materials, such as coal, oil and iron; finished products such as

TABLE 1.3

Population, Income per Capita and its Growth Rate for 12 Regions

Regions	1957 Population (millions)	Income per capita, 1957 $	Rate of increase in income per head, 1950–1960, % p.a.
A: DEVELOPED «CAPITALIST» COUNTRIES			
A 1 North America and Australia	200	1993	1.5
A 2 E.E.C.	166	911	4.7
A 3 Other European countries	86	1123	2.6
A 4 Other countries	107	425	7.5
B: EUROPEAN «COMMUNIST» COUNTRIES			
B 1 Soviet Union	200	605	8.7
B 2 Rest of Eastern Europe	114	508	7.5
C: LESS DEVELOPED COUNTRIES			
C 1 Communist Asia	666	102	8.6
C 2 Africa	172	143	1.6
C 3 Non-comm. Asia	733	147	1.7
C 4 Latin America	185	312	1.4
C 5 Oil-producing countries	39	320	3.9
C 6 Mediterranean	138	355	1.3

clothing, houses and transport equipment; and services, such as the traffic of goods, the distribution of consumer goods, the cinema or ladies hairdressing; and an enormous number of semi-finished intermediary products. If we want to get an idea of the total quantity of goods produced by a country, we may calculate the total net value produced, or *national product*. In order to yield comparable figures, the value of each product has to be calculated by applying the same prices in all countries, e.g. the price a commodity had, in a certain period, in the United States. We sometimes call such figures «real» values, as against the «nominal» figures, calculated in terms of each country's current prices.

Colin Clark, the well-known British statistician, who has made many investigations in this field, has expressed the production of all countries in the amount of dollars [on an average] for which these goods could be bought in the United States during the period 1925–1934 [i.e. a period with five prosperous years and five years of depression[1]].

The quantity of goods worth one dollar in that period he calls an International Unit [I.U.]. When calculating the net value of production we have – apart from some complications which will not interest the layman – to deduct the value of goods absorbed by the production process, such as imported raw materials, worn-out parts of machines, etc. The result of our calculation is called the real net geographical product [in 1925/34 dollars] or real income from home production. [Of course the use of other units than the I.U. would also be permitted.] Income from home production is, for all countries, by far the largest part of national income, which includes also income from other sources, such as foreign investment. Real income from home production calculated per head appears to differ greatly for the different countries. Colin Clark states that, calculated per head of the population and assuming everyone is working 2500 hours per year, income, in I.U., was in 1925/29:

TABLE 1.4

Real Income per 2500 Hours of Work, in I.U. 1925/29

United States	590
Canada	550
United Kingdom	502
Netherlands	357
Germany and Austria	292
Poland	117
Russia	95
India [incl. Pakistan, Burma and Ceylon]	64
China [incl. Korea and Formosa]	44

1. COLIN CLARK, *The Economics of 1960*, London, 1942.

7

Current figures being calculated by the United Nations are, in various respects, more accurate but, in other respects, less appropriate for our purpose; although they also illustrate the lack of homogeneity in world economy. Such figures are, e.g., the figures of national income per head expressed in one currency, namely dollars. They are not directly comparable since they disregard price differences; but the differences in prices are much less than those in incomes and, therefore, they still have some illustrative power. The most recent of these figures have been used in table 1.3.

1.5 – It has already been observed that there are various *reasons* for these differences. One reason is the difference in *capital per head and land per head* available for production. The low figure for China, e.g., is partly connected with the fact that in that country only about 4 acres [1.6 hectare] is available per farmer. This makes it necessary to follow methods of production which lead to a much lower return than would otherwise have been obtained. Moreover, the quantity of capital goods, i.e. agricultural machinery, cattle, etc., per head is very low. All in all, the Chinese farmer produces only a fraction of what his American colleague produces.

As already noted, the extent of the quantitative influence of the various factors is not yet known quite exactly. Some investigations suggest that the influence of capital per head is rather important; an increase of 1 per cent of capital per head may yield an increase in product per head of $\frac{1}{4}$ or $\frac{1}{3}$ per cent [P. Douglas].

It has become customary, in recent years, to use the concept of the «*capital coefficient*» or *capital-output ratio*, i.e. the ratio between the total capital of a country and its total income, or, as the case may be, between an increase in capital and the accompanying increase in income. The former ratio may be called the average capital coefficient; the latter the marginal capital coefficient. Since the increase in capital over a certain period represents the country's net investments, the marginal capital coefficient may also be defined as the ratio of net investment to the increase in income. The numerical values of capital coefficients for nations as a whole are known very crudely only and are between 3 and 6. It is interesting to note that they do not show, in countries for which older statistics are available, very much change over the last century. It should be kept in mind that the increase in income need not necessarily be caused by an increase in capital alone.

It is obvious that, within certain bounds at least, an increase in land available per head will also tend to increase production per head. Formulated in another way, population density will affect productivity, and hence welfare, in an inverse way. There is some difference of opinion about this point. It is sometimes maintained that the relation is more complicated and that, up to certain densities, an increase in population density will increase productivity; since in the end the opposite tendency will prevail, there will be at least one point in which productivity is a maximum. This point of density is called the optimum density or *optimum population* point. The reason why – up to that point – an increase in density may be favourable to productivity may be that certain activities can be organized more efficiently. This will be true for industries where mass production is much more productive than small-scale production; it will also be true, e.g., for the transportation of commodities. Whether these tendencies are important enough to counteract the opposite tendencies in the other industries has so far hardly been investigated. The impression of the present author, obtained from a crude statistical analysis, is that the optimum is very near to the lowest densities registered for countries as a whole. Therefore, by far the larger part of world population is living in countries with more than an optimum population.

The results of investigations as to the influence of another important factor, the *innate skill* of the population, are contradictory. On the one hand, it is reported that rather primitive populations can easily be trained in modern industrial activities. On the other hand, it is only too well known that the business sense of several oriental populations is very little developed, leading to a pronounced indifference towards increasing their standards of living as soon as some customary level has been reached. One should be careful, however, not to confuse the consequences of a lack of capital or land with those of the innate personal abilities of the population. The apparent «backward» methods of the Chinese farmer, for example, are to a great extent a result of a lack of equipment; in the given circumstances they still yield the best return.

Lack of capital and other resources can easily explain the huge differences in *training* between the wealthier and the poorer regions of the world. Training in all its different forms represents an investment in human beings and as such tends to be low wherever resources are modest. The importance of training for the level of productivity of a country has recently been illustrated by estimates made by Professor Edward F. Denison[1]. Of the total annual rise in real income per head of 1.60 per cent [between 1929 and 1957] in the United States, Denison attributes 0.67 per cent to increased education. In this figure the influence of «technical progress» or «the advance of knowledge», as he expresses it, is not included and makes for another 0.58 per cent increase. This implies that in these more recent investigations relatively less influence is attributed to the increase in material capital per capita.

Recently, some attempts have been made to measure the influence of the various incentives characterizing the organization of the economy. The impression exists that the stimulus given by free competition is very powerful and has been underestimated by progressive politicians. The «social climate» or the «industrial relations», the human relations between management and workers, are also of considerable importance.

1.6 – The total product of a country is, finally, spread over the various *groups of the population* by means of a process of exchange. The proportions going to labour, capital and land are not always known very exactly, although an increasing number of investigations have recently been published. As far as our information goes, there is the curious tendency for these proportions to be about the same under very different conditions. This is true, in particular, of the distribution of income in the United Kingdom and the United States during the last half of the nineteenth and the first quarter of the twentieth century. Within certain limits this stability holds true for a number of other countries and for recent years, but there is a tendency for labour income to rise more rapidly than the other incomes. The ratios observed for the period just stated were 70 per cent for labour, 20–25 per cent for capital and 5–10 per cent for landowners. The relative constancy of these figures implies that in periods or countries where one of the factors is scarce its remuneration per unit is very high in

1. EDWARD F. DENISON, «*The Sources of Economic Growth in the United States and the Alternatives Before Us*», Supplementary Paper No. 13, Committee for Economic Development, New York, January 1962.

comparison to other periods or countries. Capital income per unit of capital was much higher in 1850 in the United States than in 1910 or 1940; labour income per hour of work was very much lower in 1850 than it is nowadays. Labour income is also much lower in China than in France; and much lower in France than in the United States, according to the different relative scarcities of labour in these countries.

1.7 – Between these national economic units of so widely differing a character there are *various forms of economic intercourse*. These may, for the sake of convenience, be roughly subdivided as follows:
[1] Exchange of products against products, i.e. current trade in commodities or goods and services;
[2] Transfer of factors of production, i.e. of [a] persons, or migration, [b] land, which occurs as a consequence of changes in territory, and [c] capital, known as capital exports and imports.
  From the economic point of view [b] is not a common form of intercourse, but a consequence of political events. If it occurs, it is accompanied by transfers of type [2a] and [2c]. After 1914 [2a] did not take place to any appreciable extent either, in contrast to what happened in earlier periods. By far the most important forms of intercourse are those under [1] and [2c]. In the following chapters we will consider each of these forms of intercourse more closely. In addition, we shall study their financial aspects.

2 – CURRENT TRANSACTIONS

2.1 – When speaking of current transactions between countries we are thinking of *imports* and *exports* of products, i.e. *goods and services,* and not of factors of production. An example of such trade is the export from tropical areas of cotton, cane sugar, coffee, cocoa, coprah etc. to the temperate zones and the import, by the former, of textiles, machinery, ships and motor cars. From countries with rich ore deposits, iron, copper, zinc and many other metals flow in a continuous stream to other regions; agricultural districts ship their butter, cheese, meat, hides and wool; horticultural areas supply fruits and vegetables. From these examples, the underlying reason for these transactions – to be discussed more fully later – may already be clear. One country, in view of its climate, the special skill of its population or its capital resources, is a more appropriate supplier of one type of goods; another country is better equipped to supply another kind of goods. There will be even more reason to convey such goods along vast distances if they are of high value in proportion to their transport costs. Very heavy goods of comparatively little value, such as coal, iron ore or potatoes, will in general not be transported very far; they seldom cross the oceans [cf. diagram 2.11].

For every commodity there is a certain maximum distance [varying slightly according to circumstances] beyond which it can hardly be shipped competitively. Generally speaking, therefore, large countries have smaller imports and exports in proportion to total production than small countries. This is illustrated by diagram 2.12, which gives a survey of the international trade of the principal countries compared with their national incomes. In the column of imports one can compare the relative importance of the different countries for world trade, while every horizontal quadrangle gives an idea of the ratio between imports and national income for each country. Therefore, although a country such as the U.S.A. is of great importance to world trade, its imports are quite small when compared with its national income.

DIAGRAM 2.11

Composition of World Trade [T] in and World Production [P] of the Principal Basic Products [1936/7]

$T\,[1936]$	$P\,[1937]$

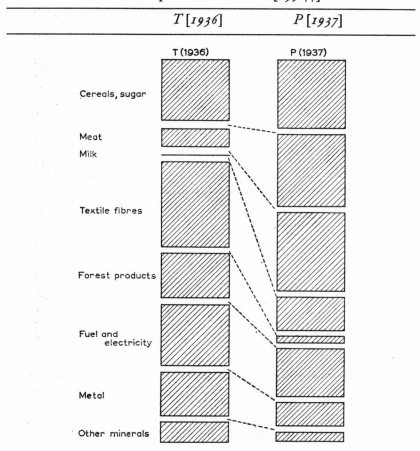

Goods, difficult to transport, such as milk, play a much smaller part in international trade than in international production; for easily transportable and specifically high-value goods, such as textile fibres, it is just the other way about.

The influence of distance on the choice of supplies is illustrated by the map on page 15.

From this map one can see that the share of any supplying country [in this case, U.S., U.K. or Germany] in the imports of the importing

DIAGRAM 2.12

National Income and Imports of a Number of Countries, 1930

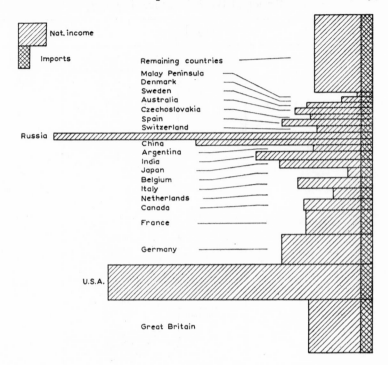

The parts of the right-hand column show the significance of each of the countries to world trade. The two quadrangles in each horizontal bar show the extent of the imports of the country concerned with respect to the national income of that country.

country is higher for near-by than for far-away importing countries. Exceptions to this rule are found among the countries mainly importing from the United Kingdom, since the Commonwealth ties sometimes determine the choice of supplier rather than costs or distance [as an element of costs].

Recent studies[1] have shown that the total commodity exports e_{AB}

1. Cf. J. TINBERGEN, *Shaping the World Economy*, New York, 1962, p. 262 ff. Slightly different results have been obtained by P. PÖYHÖNEN and K. PULLIAINEN («*Toward a General Theory of International Trade*» and «*A World Trade Study: an Econometric Model of the Pattern of the Commodity Flows in International Trade in 1948–1960*», Ekonomiska Samfundets Tidskrift 1963 : 2, pp. 69 ff and 78 ff).

(per cent of total imports from these three countries)
into all countries of the world

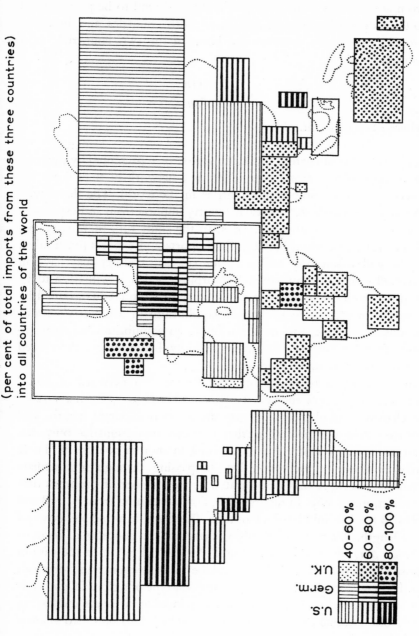

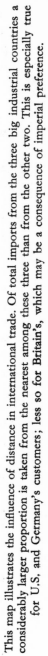

40 – 60 %

60 – 80 %

80 – 100 %

U.K.

Germ.

U.S.

This map illustrates the influence of distance in international trade. Of total imports from the three big industrial countries a considerably larger proportion is taken from the nearest among these three than from the other two. This is especially true for U.S. and Germany's customers; less so for Britain's, which may be a consequence of imperial preference.

15

from any country A to any other country B tend to be proportional to the national incomes y_A and y_B of both countries and inversely proportional to the distance d_{AB} between the two countries; in a formula:

$$e_{AB} = c \frac{y_A y_B}{d_{AB}}$$

where c is a constant.

2.2 – The flow of current transactions may be represented by the total *money value of these transactions*. There is a network of such flows between the large number of countries in the world. The flows will, as a rule, be *multilateral*, i.e. each country imports from and exports to a large number of other countries. In the short run, there is no necessity for equilibrium between the imports and exports [both taken in the widest sense] of any one country; each country may have an «overall» deficit or an «overall» surplus. A deficit will have to be paid for from the reserves of the country or from credits granted by other countries. Even if there is equilibrium in a country's transactions as a whole, this does not imply an equilibrium between imports from and exports to any other individual country; there need not be «*bilateral* equilibrium».

In order better to understand the nature of a network of flows, we can imagine how such a network could be built up from a number of elements. As elements we may use flows of different length. The shortest flow conceivable is that between two countries only, i.e. starting in one country A and finishing in another country B. There may be flows of increasing length, passing through intermediate stations; the *length* may be indicated by the number of countries they connect, minus one. In diagram 2.2, flow 2, running from A to B and from B to C, would have a length 2. There are, in principle, flows of any length. We may, in addition, introduce the concepts of *closed* or *circular flows* or *circuits* [flow 3] and *open flows* [flow 4]. In the case of closed flows the starting country and the finishing country are identical; with open flows they are not. The simplest type of a closed flow is one of length 2, ending in the same country in which it starts and having only one intermediate station [flow 5]; it will also be called *bilateral equilibrium flow*.

DIAGRAM 2.2

Composition of a Network of Flows from Elementary Flows

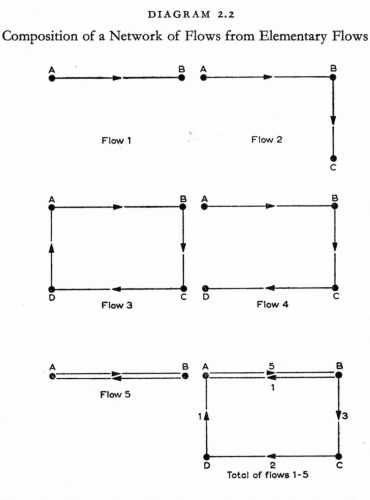

1: Flow of length 1; 2: flow of length 2; 3: closed or circular flow of length 4;
4: open flow of length 3; 5: closed flow of length 2 [bilateral equilibrium flow].

All these elementary flows may be of different *strength* or *width* [i.e. in our case, money value].

In order that a network of flows be a complete *equilibrium network*, i.e. that for each country total imports are equal to total exports, it should be composed only of closed flows. A network may be an *incomplete* equilibrium network, if equilibrium exists only for a certain group of countries; then open flows also would be permitted, provided that they start and end outside the group.

While a network can be built up from its elements in only one way, the decomposition of a given network into simpler flows is not an easy operation and is not an unambiguous one either. Different alternative sets of circular flows may lead to one and the same network and hence the network may be decomposed in different ways. Only the bilateral equilibrium flows can be determined in an unequivocal way by taking, of the two total flows between any two countries, the smaller of the two and adding one of equal size but opposite direction to that smaller one. After deducing these bilateral equilibrium flows from the original flows one obtains the bilateral surplus flows, which are the sum total of the open flows and the circular flows with a length above 2. If a country is not in equilibrium, its «net position» will be equal to the sum total of all open flows which start or finish in that country.

The concepts just introduced are of some importance for the organization of payments between a set of countries [cf. ch. 4].

The geographical structure of world trade is illustrated by the following figures which indicate the intensity of the total flows between any of the four areas distinguished [table 2.2]. It will be clear that the net positions of each area can be found by comparing their import total [bottom row] and their export total [last column]. The bilateral equilibrium components are 5.1 between Western Europe and North America, 2.6 between Western Europe and Latin America, 3.6 between North America and Latin America, etc. Trade between Europe and North America and trade within these areas, together cover half of the world trade.

2.3 – In the organization of trade three states may be distinguished: it may be [i] completely *free*, i.e. not subject to any permit or payment; or it may be [ii] *hampered* by one or more of such impediments, in a more or less arbitrary way; or, finally it may be [iii] *controlled*, i.e. completely subject to permits. The first state has hardly ever existed in a pure form, but it was approached during the last century and a half by a number of countries following a free-trade policy. In scientific discussions free trade plays an important role [cf. below]. The state of complete control, meaning that all trans-

TABLE 2.2

Trade Flows in 1960 between the main Areas of the World [in Milliards of Dollars] [1]

| Exporting Area | Destination [2] | | | | | | | | |
	NA	WE	Jap	LA	Ov.£	Non-£ M.E., Asia	Rest	Comm.	Total
North America	6.8	7.8	1.5	3.6	2.5	1.4	0.3	0.2	24.2
Western Europe	5.1	29.1	0.4	2.6	6.2	2.3	2.8	2.5	51.2
Japan	1.2	0.5	.	0.3	1.0	0.9	0.1	0.1	4.1
Latin America	3.7	2.7	0.2	0.7	0.2	0.7	1.6	0.3	8.5
Overseas £ Area	1.7	6.0	1.0	0.2	2.9	0.7	0.1	0.6	13.4
Non-£ M.E. and Asia	0.9	2.2	0.5	0.1	1.2	0.4	0.1	0.4	5.8
Rest of World	0.5	2.2	0.0	0.1	0.1	0.0	0.2	0.0	3.2
Communist Countries	0.1	2.6	0.1	0.2	0.5	0.5	0.1	10.9	15.1
Total	19.9	53.0	3.8	7.8	14.5	6.1	4.4	15.0	125.5

1. Source: *International Trade,* 1960, GATT, Geneva, 1961.
2. For meaning of abbreviations, see first column.

actions are subject to government decisions, is to be found in the countries of the communist block and is approached by other countries in war-time. Under these circumstances that control will be directed on the basis of some general program or plan derived from the aims of economic policy in general. The intermediate form of «hampered» trade is the one existing in most non-communist countries at present; it is applied somewhat more occasionally and as a corrective to free trade. The very fact that such impediments are subject to frequent unco-ordinated changes makes them appear to be more arbitrary than the restrictions under the state of complete control. In both cases the foreign trader feels that he lacks any certainty or influence as to vital aspects of his existence.

The «permits» [under complete control] may be based either on a system of *quantitative restrictions* or *quotas* or on a system of *currency restrictions*; the payments to be made are usually *import duties*, and other incidental payments. Quantitative restrictions are imposed if only a certain quantity and no more of a certain commodity is admitted per year; currency restrictions make available a limited amount of certain types of foreign currency [e.g. dollars]. To the trader who does not get his import permit it hardly matters what the basis is; both restrictions restrict trade. Quantitative restrictions are also sometimes applied to exports. Usually this happens in times of a scarcity of goods, whereas the tendency to restrict imports prevails in times of a scarcity of foreign currency or severe competition. « Payments » sometimes may take the form of extra payments to obtain foreign currency, meaning that a concealed devaluation is ap-

TABLE 2.3

Average Import Duties on a Number of Commodity Groups for 14 Countries [or Areas][1]

	A	DK	N	P	S	CH	GB
Chemicals	13	4	10	23	5	6	10[4]
Paper	16	6	8	24	6	19	13
Textiles[2]	20	9	15	74	12	10	23
Machinery[3]	18	6	10	14	9	6	17
Electr. Mach.	21	8	13	21	10	5	23

	BNL	F	D	I	EEC	USA	CDN
Chemicals	7	16	8	17	12	24	11
Paper	14	16	8	18	15	10.5	17
Textiles[2]	14	19	11	20	16	26	21
Machinery[3]	8	18	5	20	13	12	9
Electr. Mach.	11	19	6	21	15	20	18

1. Source: PEP [Political and Economic Planning], *Atlantic Tariffs and Trade,* London, 1962. Symbols used for countries are international motor car symbols: A = Austria; DK = Denmark; N = Norway; P = Portugal; S = Sweden; CH = Switzerland; GB = United Kingdom; BNL = Benelux; F = France; D = Germany; I = Italy; EEC = European Economic Community [Common Market]; USA = United States of America; CDN = Canada.

2. Yarns, fabrics and made-up articles.
3. Other than electrical.
4. Bulk of imports.

plied; there may also sometimes be export duties. There also exist «compensatory duties» to be paid on imports, if the commodity considered is taxed inside the country by an excise or a custom. In the latter case the intention of the compensatory duty is the equal treatment of foreign and home producers.

Whereas quantitative restrictions were severe during the Great Depression and shortly after World War II, they are now less important – at least between members of the Organization for Economic Co-operation and Development [OECD]. Current quantitative restrictions affect less than 10 per cent of the total trade between these countries. Import duties are still considerable in a number of countries; some figures are presented in table 2.3.

There may be blocks of countries with free internal trade and with a *common tariff* for the outside world or without such a common tariff. In the first case we speak of a «customs union». The German countries formed such a union in the latter part of the 19th century. Belgium and Luxembourg did so after the First World War; and since 1948, Belgium, Luxembourg and the Netherlands together have formed the Benelux union. Trade between the states of the United States of America is also practically free. In cases where tariffs applied vis-à-vis the outside world are not uniform we speak of a *«free trade area»*. A customs union may develop into an *economic union* if further steps towards integration are taken. Usually, when speaking of an economic union or of integration we think of a unification of further taxes and of other aspects of economic policy. In this text we will define the state of economic integration as the economic policy which shows an *optimum of centralization* [cf. ch. 6.6]. An optimum is not necessarily a maximum; and the extent to which [and in what matters] centralization should be aimed at depends on the many elements of the problem.

2.4 – For a correct understanding of the essence of international economic relations it is useful to consider the extreme case, i.e. the one of *free trade*. In addition, when investigating the state of free trade, we will often assume that transportation costs can be neglected. For low value goods this is not possible and sometimes, therefore, we will try to take account of the consequences of transportation costs. Disregarding transportation costs, we may state that, under free trade, prices of one and the same commodity will be *equal in all countries*. Another characteristic of free trade is that it is *multilateral*: if there are no difficulties in paying for trade transactions, it would be pure co-incidence if there were bilateral equilibrium between any two countries [cf. 2.2]. Thus, a country may have, and usually will have, deficits with some and surpluses with other countries.

Free trade is not equivalent to what the economist calls free competition. Free or perfect competition has become the scientific term for competition between a large number of competitors, where no single competitor feels able to influence the price level of the market by his acts. Competition is called imperfect if one or more of the competitors are able to influence prices, i.e. if there are monopolistic elements in the market. In international as well as national trade, market imperfections are very common; they may be caused by natural and other monopolistic factors. One of the competitors may have a natural monopoly by finding himself close to his customers; or his product may have special features which the other producers are unable to supply completely. Consequently, international trade appears at least in the short run to show somewhat the characteristics of *imperfect competition*. This is demonstrated by the so-called short-term elasticity of a country's share in world trade with respect to its relative price level. A fall in a country's export price level relative to the export price level of all countries together of, say, one per cent appears to be followed – in the first year or so – by an increase in that country's share in world exports by no more than 2 per cent. The figure 2 in this case represents the elasticity just mentioned. In the case of perfect competition it should have been, theoretically, infinite. It is often even less than 2. The same applies to the short-term elasticity of imports as a ratio to total home demand with respect to the ratio of import prices to home price level. Both tendencies are connected, it seems, with the difficulty of switching from one supplier to another because of market imperfections. It is natural to expect [and probable] that the long-term elasticities are higher; and the same applies to the elasticities pertaining to one single commodity, especially staples[1]. In this context, by short-term reactions we mean

1. For a recent study of this problem, cf. R. M. STERN, «*British and American Productivity and Comparative Costs in International Trade*», Oxford Economic Papers, New Series, Vol. 14, No. 3, Oct. 1962, p. 275.

reactions taking no more than one or two years. Therefore, although free trade does not necessarily imply free competition, we will, in theoretical analysis, often assume them to co-exist.

2.5 – International trade may be said to be a consequence of a certain *division of labour:* if everybody produced by himself everything he consumes there would be no trade. The basis of this division of labour is that there are differences in the *relative* efficiency of the same industries between countries. Each country is endowed with different factors of production. However, to start with, let us only speak of labour and later expand our argument so as to include other productive contributions. With free trade and neglecting transportation costs, there will be one single price on the world market for each product. We choose the units of these products so as to have a price of $ 1 for each commodity. The efficiency of each industry in each country may now be indicated by the quantity produced in one hour. Let us suppose that we have two countries and two industries only, and let their efficiencies be given in the following matrix:

DATA FOR A VERY SIMPLE MODEL OF INTERNATIONAL TRADE

	Quantity produced by one man-hour:	
	Product 1	*Product 2*
Country 1	1	0.91
Country 2	0.42	0.50

Under these circumstances it is clear that country 1 would be wise to produce only product 1 and country 2 only product 2. A man-hour used by country 1 in industry 2 would yield only $ 0.91 of value, whereas one man-hour in industry 1 yields $ 1.—. If country 1 wants to consume product 2, it can obtain one unit of it by producing commodity 1 and exporting it, buying commodity 2 with the proceeds. For country 2 a man-hour used in industry 2 will yield $ 0.50 of value, and, by exchanging it on the world market, $\frac{1}{2}$ unit of 1 may be obtained which is more than would be obtained by producing commodity 1 directly. What is important is that relative – not absolute – efficiencies are decisive. Country 1 is more efficient, in absolute terms, than country

2 in producing commodity 2; but, nevertheless, it should not produce commodity 2. The above reasoning will have made this clear. In addition, it should be observed that although country 1 produces more units of «2» per man-hour than does country 2, it does not produce it more cheaply. Wages will be much higher in country 1 than in country 2. If there is perfect competition between employers, wages will be almost $ 1.— per hour in country 1 and almost $ 0.50 in country 2. Our little model could be extended to deal with more industries, more countries, and more factors of production without changing the basic conclusions as to what products will be exported and what the level of wages [and other incomes] will be. This illustrates what is called the «*theory of comparative cost*» [cf. also appendix 1].

Similarly, somewhat more complicated propositions may be made on the «division of labour» between a larger number of countries, or a larger number of products, or a larger number of factors of production. With more factors of production, the tendency will be to produce as high a total value of production as possible with the help of all factors available. It will be possible to use all units of all factors [say labour, land and capital] only if either [i] the proportion in which these factors are needed is the same for all products and for the country as a whole, or [ii], when this is not so, if there is a sufficient «spread» in these proportions for the various goods. The meaning of this latter condition may be clarified by a simple example of two factors only: labour and land. If a country has 100 units of labour for every unit of land and products exist which, respectively, require 50 and 150 units of labour in combination with one unit of land, it will be possible for the country by producing equal quantities of both products to use both factors fully. If, however, the only products known have the proportions 50 : 1 and 75 : 1, the country concerned will not be able to use all its labour. We call this a case of «absolute» shortage of land; it will not present itself if, in the process of production, there is an unlimited possibility of replacing one factor by the other.

2.6 – We are now approaching the *fundamental thesis of the doctrine of free trade* which, for a long time, determined discussions on trade policy and [in a way] still does. It states that, *under certain conditions, free trade leads to maximum welfare*. Understanding the conditions is just as important as knowing the thesis itself. The major conditions are:

[1] All productive resources are used in production, i.e. there are *no idle resources* [unemployed workers or idle capacity] except for «absolute» shortages in some other factors.

[2] Prices of products are equal to their *marginal costs,* i.e. to the cost of producing the last unit.

[3] The temporary consequences of adaptations of productive resources to changes in demand are ignored.

[4] Welfare is measured by the *total value of production at free-trade prices.* This method of measuring welfare is only one of several; one might also use the total value of *expenditure* [for consumption and investment] at free-trade prices. It is also significant to note that welfare is assumed to be independent of the distribution of production over individuals or groups of the population.

Under the above conditions it is easy to prove the thesis. A system of free trade implies that every country is using its productive resources in the most efficient way, as was illustrated by our little model. Alternative uses would be those resulting from some form of protection or from another method of pricing. They would always result in using the resources in a less efficient way; in our example the use of labour in industry 2 by country 1, or the use of labour in industry 1 by country 2. The interesting point to note is that not only would total welfare decline, but also the welfare of any one country involved. Therefore, if protection is an advantage for some groups of the population, it must at the same time be a disadvantage for other groups of the same population. This latter part of the proposition only applies, however, as long as we measure welfare by the value of production at free-trade prices. If we measured it by the value of expenditure at free-trade prices it would no longer be valid for countries *large enough to be able to influence their terms of trade,* i.e. the ratio of prices at which they import and export. Indeed, large countries may, by imposing a tariff, depress the demand for some import products and so get them, as a nation, cheaper than without such a tariff. Moreover, they might apply tariffs in such a way as to maximize the volume of goods that they obtain by production and trade. The tariff which makes this volume a maximum has been called the *«optimum tariff».* The optimum of course refers to the country concerned. Since the imposition of any tariff always decreases the total value of production of the world at large, any advantages obtained by a country would be at the expense of other countries. There may be cases where this might by itself be a positive contribution to welfare, if welfare is also to imply certain aspects of *distribution*. The same advantage to the first country might, however, have been reached also in other ways; i.e., by producing according to a free-trade régime and by subsidizing that country.

Marginal cost pricing may not be possible in some industries, without subsidizing them. If marginal costs are below average costs, this method of pricing would imply permanent losses to the industry concerned. Marginal costs should be taken to mean long-term marginal costs, however, and then it is doubtful whether there are many industries for which these are lower than average costs. But some industries do show this feature as a consequence of *indivisibilities in their equipment*. In countries with small markets they are more numerous than in big countries. For these industries certain types of subsidies would be preferable to protection – from a purely economic point of view, i.e. disregarding possible difficulties of administrative organization. Subsidies are preferable if they leave prices equal to the free-competition prices. It can be proved that the latter maximize welfare; the use made of productive resources would yield a higher utility.

Full use of resources has also been mentioned as a condition for the validity of the free trade doctrine. If there are unemployed resources, tariffs may contribute to their fuller use and so increase production. For practical political purposes, this condition may be interpreted to mean that the full advantages of free trade [through the division of labour] can only be reaped if the full use of resources is maintained by an appropriate full employment policy [or, at least, high and stable employment] [ch. 7]. For countries with an absolute shortage of another factor such a policy may, however, be impossible.

2.7 – The propositions so far discussed have all referred to *long-term adaptations*. As was expressed in our condition [3], temporary consequences of adaptations may be ignored if the advantages to be obtained are of a lasting character. In reality, the problems of temporary adaptation do count; especially since they represent disadvantages that have to be suffered before any advantages will be observable. Therefore, an *optimum policy* leading from a state of protection towards one of free trade will have to be taken so as to maximize *net* advantages [discounted over time in some acceptable way]. Here, net advantages are the advantages obtained from free trade minus the disadvantages of adaptation, such as the cost of retraining workers and of extra investments.

Thus, protection may be acceptable for periods of adaptation to new circumstances. It may even be acceptable if it did not exist previously, if import duties are the simplest device temporarily to support an industry whose sudden disappearance would be too great a shock to the economy.

The same argument applies to the use of import duties in order to support an «*infant industry*». In this case, one could say that protection aids in raising the efficiency of that industry, and that it, therefore, represents a case where efficiency is not given beforehand, as in our matrix in section 2.5. It remains to be seen, however, whether the same effect cannot be obtained by subvention instead of protection. The danger of protection lies in its «invisibility» to the public and to the tax-payer. Thus there exists the tendency to maintain it and to inhibit the wholesome forces of competition on less productive units.

2.8 – After a *period of isolation* as, for example, created by a war, the liberalization of a country's trade presents a subtle problem. It will have to be solved gradually and with great care in order to prevent the sudden disruption of the many partial equilibria on which a war economy is built, before the conditions for general equilibrium are fulfilled. The conditions of such a general equilibrium will be discussed in chapter 4. Only some examples of the problems involved can be mentioned here. Before liberalizing foreign trade in a certain commodity, the home market should be more or less in equilibrium, which may be tested by the abolition of rationing, if it exists. There is no point in liberalizing trade if there still is rationing; and the controls needed for rationing are even in direct contradiction to free trade. Before any more general liberalization of imports is undertaken, it is necessary to be sure that the general price level inside the country is competitive on the world market; otherwise there is a real danger that imports will grow very fast and surpass exports.

Liberalization of trade will generally also mean the disruption of bilateral equilibria with individual countries which are likely to exist as a consequence of unequal softness of the currencies in war-time. Therefore, there should be parallelism between steps towards freer trade and steps towards convertibility of currencies [cf. chs. 8 and 9].

2.9 – In an attempt to restore free trade, various alternative methods may be followed. These will be discussed in more detail in chapter 8. One of the so-called partial forms of integration is the establishment, as already mentioned, of a customs union between a limited number of countries. It is an interesting question as to whether such a *customs union does or does not represent a useful step towards world free trade.* While it is clear that, in the end, if world free trade is to be reached, all countries will have to follow the steps taken by the members of a customs union, doubt may arise as to the contribution the latter makes to the best division of labour. In fact, a customs union will probably improve, in some ways, the division of labour. If shoes can be made more cheaply in Holland and glass more cheaply in Belgium, elimination of trade barriers between these two countries may contribute to a more rational production pattern. However, the existence of a tariff at the external frontier of the union may also lead to an erroneous increase in, say, butter production in Holland, even if the cheaper potential supplier would have been Denmark. A happy formulation of these two aspects of a partial customs union has been Viner's distinction between the *trade-creating* elements and the *trade-diverting* elements of a union. It very much depends on the data of the actual situation whether one or the other aspect is more important.

3 – INTERNATIONAL MOVEMENTS OF FACTORS: LAND, LABOUR AND CAPITAL

3.1 – As observed in chapter 1 [cf. 1.7], products may not be the only object of economic intercourse between nations. To a lesser degree, there also exist movements of factors. They will be briefly discussed in this chapter.

Movements of *land,* in the literal sense of the word, are, of course, impossible. However, the transfer of territory from one nation to another may occur; and this sometimes has assumed considerable dimensions. As examples, one may recall the cases of Austria, Yugoslavia and Rumania after the First World War, the history of Poland and the Baltic States and the reduction in German territory after the Second World War. The common characteristic of all these examples is their political, rather than normal economic nature. Of course, considerable increases in territory have also occurred in colonial areas, by means which cannot now be considered to be very different from the ones previously mentioned. The more satisfactory cases of any extent are the examples of the exploration and consequent use of newly discovered empty territories, as was virtually the case in the United States. The creation of new land by reclamation represents the most attractive form of land occupation, since not even the slightest chance of depriving other peoples of their resources is involved; but its extent has so far been very modest. And, in a way, we are moving away from the concept of movement of factors between nations if we speak of these one-sided additions to territory.

Transfer of territory is, in any case, not now considered a normal element of international economic policy.

3.2 – Movements of *labour,* i.e. of population, known as *migration,* have been important, especially for certain areas of immigraton, where they constituted the larger part of the increase in population during some periods. This was particularly true in the case of the United States of America between 1850 and 1914, when some 30 millions moved to that country. For the countries from which these emigrants moved the significance of the decrease in population pressure was usually only modest: the largest percentage of a population that ever emigrated in one year was a little above 1 per cent.

Since 1914 the extent of international migration has been very much reduced. The reason is obvious: it is a disadvantage to the workers in an immigration territory if workers come in from poorer countries and increase the supply of labour, and, consequently, depress the wage level. This conclusion would be erroneous if the United States had in fact a population below the optimum population [cf. ch. 1]. But there are reasons to doubt that proposition. This opposition to immigration constitutes a serious example of a conflict of interests between the workers of a wealthy territory and those of the rest of the world. In general, it may be said to be to the advantage of world production if labour is transferred from countries where its productivity is low to countries where it is high. Thus, this conflict is a tragic one. Its solution is hampered by the fact that the supply of labour in the overpopulated areas in the Far East is so endless that the American worker does not see a solution in the admission of immigrants unless at the same time some prospect exists of limiting the supply of labour. In India the government has officially recognized the importance of «*family planning*» and, thus, a beginning of understanding for this aspect of the problem has been shown. It is to be hoped that, at a later stage, the less populated areas will be prepared to revise their immigration policy, under certain guarantees to the effect that a check to population increases is being applied.

3.3 – In recent times, and in fact ever since the middle of the nineteenth century, the most important form of the international movements of factors has, from the economic point of view, been represented by *capital movements*. These may take the form of loans granted by one country to another, upon which regular amortizations and interest have to be paid, or the form of participations, on which there is no amortization, but on which dividends are paid. Loans may be subdivided into short-term and long-term. For the process of production long-term loans and participations are the more important types: they come down, in real terms, to the transfer, from one country to another of commodity stocks of either a durable or non-durable character. Durable commodities like railway equipment, machinery, etc., make it possible to create productive enterprises, and non-durable supplies put the latter into operation. Once in operation, they will be able to pay their workers from the proceeds of their production. The non-durable supplies are necessary to bridge the gap between the moment when operation starts and the moment when sales are at their normal level. The payments of interest and amortization or of dividends represent an annual «mortgage» on the part of the increased production, which, in the case of a productive investment, can actually be borne. Usually, the lending area will be one of the highly developed nations and the borrowing area one of the less developed areas. Capital is flowing, in such a case, from countries where it is less productive to countries where it is more productive. In this way, these movements of capital contribute to decreasing the inequality of living standards. Whether the process has ever been sufficient to stop the growing divergence of living standards is doubtful. In order to do so, these movements would probably have to be much more important[1].

Table 3.3 illustrates the amount of capitals invested abroad over the years by a number of countries.

TABLE 3.3

Foreign Assets as a Percentage of Reproducible Tangible Wealth*

Belgium	1950	12
Luxembourg	1950	— 5
Netherlands	1952	11
France	1954	4
Norway	1953	— 2
Yugoslavia	1953	— 1
Canada	1955	— 14
United States	1955	4
Australia	1956	— 6
Japan	1955	1

* Source: R. GOLDSMITH and C. SAUNDERS, ed., *The Measurement of National Wealth, Income and Wealth*, Series VIII, London, 1959, p. 14–16.

1. Cf. C. BLANCO, *The Determinants of Regional Factor Mobility*, Diss., Rotterdam, 1962; S. CHAKRAVARTY, *A Structural Study of International Capital Movements*, Netherlands Economic Institute 22/60, Rotterdam, 1960.

Private capital movements, which were an important part of total capital movements before World War I, have diminished because of increasing political uncertainty about the possibilities of receiving dividends or interest and amortization. In the colonial era there was, for a number of countries at least, almost total certainty about these transfers, whereas, in recent periods, the tendency to take autonomous decisions has increased. These decisions are partly a consequence of decreased monetary stability in the potential debtor countries and partly reflect a certain aversion towards private foreign capital.

There is another important aspect to the problem of investment in underdeveloped countries. In a number of cases such investments are not as remunerative as might have been deduced from the scarcity of capital in such countries. In other words: the efficiency of production is sometimes so low as to make such investments hardly attractive. This seems to be due, to some extent, to the absence of certain general facilities, such as energy supply, a good transportation system, reasonable housing conditions and workers with a certain minimum of training. One may speak, in this connection, of a vicious circle: if for some reason the capital stock per head is low, it is difficult to increase it. Once the circle is broken it may be easier further to increase the capital intensity. The only way to attain this higher level that seems possible is an international effort – in the *public* sphere – to supply the basic facilities in the sectors just indicated.

3.4 – *Short-term capital movements* are not able to contribute directly to the long-term increase of the equipment or the commodity stocks of a country. Their effects are, therefore, not to be expected in the commodity sphere but rather in the financial sector. Short-term credits may help to overcome temporary difficulties in the financing of foreign payments and so prevent interruptions to the smooth functioning of the economy. Thus, they may promote financial stability, i.e., in particular the maintenance of exchange rates during periods of depression, and so indirectly contribute to the development process.

4 – THE MECHANISM OF FINANCIAL TRANSACTIONS

4.1 – As we have seen, the organization of production and consumption in most countries is largely based on a far-reaching division of labour, with the consequence that there exists a complex network of transactions for which payments have to be made by various *means of payment*, which differ from country to country. The only means of payment that is accepted everywhere is *gold*. To use gold for all payments that have to be made would, however, be rather expensive in two ways: firstly, a considerable value would have to be «invested» in a country's stock of money in circulation, and, secondly, the shipment of gold to other countries involves relatively high costs of transportation, insurance etc. The use of paper money is cheaper in both respects and more convenient. However, since paper money has no intrinsic value, it has to derive its value from legal provisions which link it to a certain government. Thus, its validity is restricted to a particular country. Payments from one country to another, therefore, require a «*transfer*», i.e. transformation of home money into foreign money. This is effectuated by exchanging the various currencies against each other at a certain market price called the *exchange rate*.

In some countries there is not one single market for foreign exchange, say dollars, but the market is subdivided into compartments, each characterized by a different exchange rate for the dollar. In such a situation we speak of *multiple exchange rates*. As a rule the rates will be different for purchases of different types of goods; luxuries can only be bought at a higher dollar price than that for prime necessities [including raw materials and capital goods]. This presupposes a regulated market.

4.2 – The set of all payments made in a certain period [e.g. a year] between one country and all other countries is called that country's *balance of payments* [cf. table 4.2]. Usually this «balance» is presented in the form of one table showing, on one side, all payments made by the country and, on the other side, all payments received [the debit side and the credit side, respectively]. It may be further subdivided

TABLE 4.2

Example of Balance of Payments; United States, 1953, in Milliards of Dollars

[A equals total of 1–8, B of 9–10, C of 11–19]	Credits	Debits
A. *Goods and Services* [*net*]	*4.5*	—
1. Merchandise, Exports, f.a.s.	16.4 Imports f.a.s.	11.9
3. Foreign travel	0.5	0.9
4. Transportation	1.3	1.1
5. Insurance	..	..
6. Investment income	1.9	0.4
7. Government, n.i.e.	0.5	2.1
8. Miscellaneous	0.7	0.3
B. *Donations* [*net*]	—	*6.5*
9. Private	—	0.5
10. Official:		
10.1 Military [net]	—	4.3
10.2 Other	—	1.8
Net total [1 *through* 10.1]	—	0.2
Net total [1 *through* 10.2]	—	2.0
C. *Capital and Monetary Gold* [*net*]	*1.7*	—
11,15 Long-term liabilities [net]	0.1	—
12,16 Short-term liabilities [net]	1.0	—
13,17 Long-term assets [net]	—	0.7
14,18 Short-term assets [net]	0.2	—
19 Monetary gold	1.2	—
Net errors and omissions and mult. settlements	0.3	—

Source: *Balance of Payments Yearbook*, published by the International Monetary Fund.

into *current items*, which are payments for current transactions in goods and services, and *capital items*, being payments for property titles in the widest sense, and gold shipments. Of the current items, the payments for commodities [imports and exports] are also collectively called the *balance of trade*, whereas the payments for services, including shipping freights, interest and dividends as payments for «capital services», tourist receipts, insurance premiums, fees for free professions, etc., are summarized as the «*invisible items*». A third category, *unilateral payments* or *donations*, may occur in the balance of payments, i.e. payments not offset by commodity transactions. Well-known examples of such payments are the foreign grants received from the United States under the European Recovery Program [Marshall Plan] by European countries or development aid received by a developing country and the reparation payments made by Germany after the First World War.

4.3 – Of the various items, gold shipments are often considered to be the «*balancing item*», i.e. the item necessary to «pay for the deficit in the other items» [or, as the case may be, receivable because of a surplus in the other items]. As a first approximation, this is correct; but it should be added that sometimes also short-term capital movements of a certain type perform this function, e.g. short-term credit obtained from some international financial agency or centre. To the extent that a state of disequilibrium influences certain of the items in an automatic way, the gap may also be filled partly by changes in the other items.

If the balancing item is included it is obvious that there will always be equilibrium, which, for this reason, will be called «*formal equilibrium*». If it is not included, the phrase «balance of payments» has a different meaning. Thus conceived of, the balance of payments may or may not be in equilibrium. If it is, this balance of payments [second definition] is said to be in «*material equilibrium*». Under these circumstances, the balancing item is equal to zero. In the long run, i.e. as an average over a long period, the account must be near to material equilibrium; otherwise there would have to be a permanent accumulation of gold somewhere and a permanent drain elsewhere. However, there may be a modest deviation from material equilibrium for quite some time, e.g. if a country is gradually liquidating a large gold stock, or if a country is a gold producer. In the latter case, however, the production of gold could be considered to be a normal economic activity of the country. Thus the corresponding gold shipments might be classified as exports, which would restore material equilibrium as understood here.

4.4 – The rates of exchange against which foreign money can be obtained are not perfectly constant. In this respect, there are different systems of organization for foreign payments, some with almost completely stable rates, some with more fluctuating rates. *Stability of exchange rates* is an advantage for economic calculations; but it may be incompatible with stable prices or with long-term equilibrium in the balance of payments or with still other objectives which may be considered more desirable. Usually, systems which show very little change in rates are preferred. Occasional revisions may be necessary in the case of «fundamental disequilibrium», the term used in the Charter of the International Monetary Fund to indicate situations of more lasting disequilibrium.

A system that existed a long time and was known as the «*gold standard*» worked in about the following way. Under this system there is a fixed price against which the Central Bank buys or sells gold. For each foreign currency, say the dollar, there is one rate of exchange, say in the Netherlands f 3.60, which corresponds to this price of gold. It is called the «*mint par of exchange*». With the rate at or very near to this parity it is more advantageous to pay an American firm by buying dollars than by buying gold and shipping it, since transportation of gold is more expensive than a bank transfer. However, the rate of exchange under the gold standard was not completely stable and responded to fluctuations in demand and supply. If over a certain time unit demand for dollars surpasses their supply, the rate of exchange will rise. Payment in gold may then become relatively more attractive and beyond a certain rate definitely more attractive. This rate is called the «*upper gold point*». Conversely, if demand for dollars is low, a rate may be reached, the «*lower gold point*», where it becomes more advantageous, for Americans, to ship gold to the Netherlands. We may summarize this by saying that between the gold points gold shipments are unremunerative. Only a rigorous material equilibrium in the balance of payments will, however, keep the exchange rates within the range of the gold points. *The first line of defence* against disequilibrium is, thus, a movement of the exchange rate to one of the gold points; and the *second* consists of the automatic shipments of gold. As long as gold is shipped, the rates will remain at one of the gold points. But there is a risk of exhausting the gold stock of the weaker of the two countries if the movement goes on. This may be prevented by further lines of defence. We will speak of [a] «indirect» and [b] «direct action».

4.5 – *Indirect action,* the *third line of defence,* may again be of two types, called automatic and deliberate. *Automatic* action occurs as a consequence of the changes in monetary circulation which accompany the gold shipments. If gold is sent by the country considered [Holland] national means of circulation [notes or bank deposits] are offered to the Central Bank for the purchase of gold and so the monetary circulation is reduced. The consequence will be, in principle, a reduction in incomes, leading to reduced imports and lower prices. In principle, too, the latter will stimulate exports. However, it should be observed that this automatism does not work very strongly and quickly. Gold shipments are not usually very important in comparison with total imports and hence their influence on imports and, via prices, on exports will be small. In addition, the operation of this mechanism requires time, probably several months. It will be discussed somewhat more extensively in chapter 5.

More can be expected, in the short run, from the *deliberate* type of action, which, therefore, represents the real «third line» of defence. Its usual form under the gold standard was the raising, by the Central Bank, of the *discount rate,* i.e. the interest rate of the Bank charges for short credits [on commercial bills]. [Some other rates were usually varied at the same time.] This rate influences the other, «free» interest rates in the country and acts in two ways. First, it tends to have consequences similar to those just described for automatic action; but these, again, will only be weak and slow. Second, and this is probably the most important consequence, it will attract foreign short-term capital or prevent domestic short-term capital from being invested elsewhere. To be sure, this inflow of short-term capital will only occur if no counteracting «psychological» factors operate, i.e. if a lack of confidence in the future of the currency of the country considered

does not offset the purely economic considerations of yield. The
remedy provided by this inflow can only be a temporary one, since

DIAGRAM 4.5

An Example of Classical Discount Policy [Discount Rate of the
Netherlands Bank Between April 1935 and March 1936]

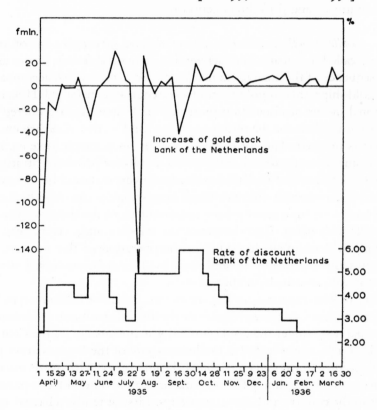

The rate is raised after every heavy fall in gold stock and lowered after a recovery
in gold holdings.

it represents a shift in the distribution of existing assets, i.e. in the
distribution of «stocks» and not a continuous flow. Therefore, it
may be an acceptable remedy for a short-term disequilibrium, but it
cannot remedy a lasting or «fundamental» disequilibrium.

The operation and results of «deliberate indirect action», or [in the usual language] of discount policy, may be seen in the example of the «defence of the Dutch guilder» during 1935/6 [cf. diagram 4.5]. Decreases of the gold stock of the Netherlands were followed by rises in the discount rate which, in their turn, led to a temporary restoration of the reserve. Nevertheless, in September 1936 the decision to devalue had to be taken, together with the only two remaining members of the «gold block», France and Switzerland.

4.6 – «*Direct action*» is the last or *fourth line of defence,* since it may be the only way of meeting a deficit, if indirect action appears to be unsuccessful or unpromising. This may be especially so in the case of a «fundamental disequilibrium», i.e. a disequilibrium in the underlying economic variables, such as the price and cost level of the country concerned.

Direct action may either consist of a change in the gold price and hence in the parity rates, or it may consist in stopping the sale of gold. In the former case the currency concerned has been *devalued.* In the latter case the old parity may be maintained, but the currency will have become *inconvertible:* the parity has then been maintained at the cost of freedom. Both of these steps will be a shock to confidence and may, therefore, disturb the financial structure of the country, at least for a short period. Central banks and governments will, thus, try to avoid them as long as possible. One of the ways to do so is by the possession of a large gold reserve. As will be discussed in chapter 5, even the largest gold stock will, however, be insufficient, if the country is in fundamental disequilibrium.

Under a situation of inconvertibility, international payments have to be regulated on a «*clearing*» basis. The simplest form of clearing possible is with respect to the payments for a bilateral equilibrium flow [cf. section 2.2]; here, a direct compensation, without any «payment», is possible. Clearing is also possible for circular flows of a greater length on a multilateral basis. For open flows the situation is even less simple. Here, evidently, clearing is only possible if the first country in such a flow grants a credit to the last country, which is then able to pay the last but one. This country can pay the last but two, and so on, until the first country obtains payment from the second in the flow. The series of payments just mentioned was made possible, under the European Recovery Program, by a chain of « drawing rights » for each of the countries concerned on its successor in the chain. No provisions are possible, in a system of clearing, for the remaining « net positions » [1].

4.7 – The « *reserve* », or « *cover* », of a currency system represents part of the assets which the Central Bank possesses against the liabilities represented by its note circulation and deposits. The remaining part of the assets usually consists of government bonds of one type or another, which are of no significance, however, as international means of payment. The reserve need not only consist of gold; for quite some time it has consisted also of silver. It is also conceivable that other commodities may be used as well. One special form that has been advocated is the system of a *« raw material standard »*, where part of the reserve would consist of warehouse bonds representing ownership of certain quantities of raw materials in a specific composition. The consequence of a raw material standard, i.e. the preparedness of central banks to buy or sell at fixed prices certain raw materials, is the stabilization of the price level of the raw materials included. Such a stabilization could contribute to the stabilization of the trade cycle, since that cycle is partly due to variations in the general price level. This is particularly true of the variations in income as calculated by many business firms, since changes in inventory prices are often wrongly considered to be an element of income. This represents the so-called « accounting error » to which the business cycle has been partly ascribed by various authors. This error would be considerably reduced by a stabilization of raw material prices.

4.8 – Usually, a system of *« flexible exchange rates »* is presented as the opposite of the « gold standard », although, in principle, the differences are not large. It operates in a similar way, but, quantitatively, the differences may be considerable. The main difference in principle is that no automatic shipment of gold applies: gold is used only by an *Exchange Equalization Fund* run by the government in order to influence exchange rates. If current demand for dollars, for example, is so

1. Cf. M. H. EKKER, « *Equilibrium of international trade and international monetary compensations* », Weltw. Archiv 64 [1950], p. 204.

much higher than the current supply of dollars as to depreciate the rate of exchange below a certain lower limit, the Fund will supply dollars or gold in order to support the rate. Conversely, it may buy dollars or gold during periods of relatively low demand. Usually, the lower and the upper limit show a much wider margin – and this is a quantitative difference – than is the case with the gold standard, e.g. 20 per cent as against perhaps 1 per cent.

However, it should not be forgotten, that there is no one single system of flexible rates or one single gold standard. Both occur in a number of alternative versions; often there has not been any system at all, especially under circumstances where disequilibrium is such that the authorities lose control of the situation. This is particularly so in the case of «*hyperinflation*». The standard case in modern Western history has been the hyperinflation in Germany in 1922 and 1923. After an initial disequilibrium, as a consequence of post-war developments [government deficits financed by money creation], demand for foreign currencies increased more and more because of speculation against the mark and of vanishing confidence in its ultimate recovery. The process resulted in a fall of its exchange rate to one billionth [in the European sense of that word, i.e. $1 : 10^{12}$] of the parity rate.

One of the functions of an Exchange Equalization Fund is the prevention and counteraction of destructive speculation. However, it can only do so if there is no fundamental disequilibrium; its function is one of bridging temporary gaps. It cannot bridge permanent gaps.

5 – DISEQUILIBRIUM AND EQUILIBRIUM IN THE BALANCE OF PAYMENTS

5.1 – In this chapter some consequences of disequilibrium in the balance of payments will be considered, the conditions for equilibrium will be formulated, and some techniques of short-term adaptations discussed.

In a state of *multilateral payments equilibrium* between nations there will be equality between the payments any country has to make to other countries and the receipts it can expect from other countries. This does not necessarily imply, as we have already stated, bilateral equilibrium between any two countries. Country A may have to pay more to country B than country B to country A; there will, then, be a deficit on the part of country A with regard to country B in their bilateral intercourse. However, if there is an «overall» equilibrium, A will have a surplus with some other country and B a deficit, and both can use their surpluses to pay for their deficits. In such a situation there will be no difficulty in declaring any currency fully convertible into any other; demand for and supply of each currency are equal to each other.

5.2 – This easy situation vanishes if the balances of payments are *not* in *equilibrium*. Even then, convertibility may be maintained for some time, if all countries are in the possession of gold or equivalent reserves. In a situation of disequilibrium there will be surplus and deficit countries. The reserves of the former will increase, and those of the latter decrease and finally be exhausted. After its reserves are exhausted, the currency of the country concerned will no longer be convertible at the existing rate of exchange. Certain portions of the demand for foreign currency can no longer be satisfied and the currency will be «*soft*» as distinguished from the «*hard*» currencies of the surplus countries. Convertibility could – perhaps – be restored if the exchange rate were lowered, i.e. if the price of one unit of that currency in terms of the others were lower. The ratio of this equilibrium rate to the actual rate may be considered to be a measure of the «degree of softness» of the currency concerned. The possibility of defining this degree depends on the existence of an equilibrium rate; we will assume that it exists, although under certain circumstances such an equilibrium rate might not be attainable in the short run. In order not to disorganize international economic intercourse completely, payments of a soft currency will have to be regulated. This means that certain demands for foreign currency will have to be curtailed by *«currency regulations»*; these are, in their material consequences, equivalent to quota systems imposed on trade. An important example of a complicated set of regulations is supplied by the monetary organization of the Sterling Area after World War II, a simplified scheme of which is given in table 5.3.

5.3 – After a *disturbance of pre-existing equilibria,* as, for example, caused by a war, a currency may be soft for some time because of a fall in the general productivity of the country or because of exceptionally high demand [as far as it is financed by inflationary means]. With the gradual restoration of productivity and of a sound internal financial situation, the question may arise as to whether convertibility can be restored, perhaps even at the pre-existing rates. For temporary disturbances this is likely to be possible; and this likelihood is one of the reasons why regulations are applied during the period of softness. Another reason may be that there is uncertainty about the existence of a short-run equilibrium rate.

In order to answer the important question of whether, under the circumstances just indicated, the moment has come to *re-establish convertibility,* we have to know the conditions which must be met for convertibility to persist. Clearly, these conditions are dependent on the exact type of convertibility envisaged. Usually, it will be, in one or more respects, *partial* convertibility which is aimed at. It may be partial in that only some groups of transactions are involved, e.g. only current transactions and not capital transactions; or it may be partial because convertibility in some other but not all other currencies is aimed at.

The main relevant condition is that there be equality between the demand for and the supply of the currencies with which convertibility is restored. This demand and supply refers to the items in the balance

TABLE 5.3

Transferability of Sterling for Direct Current Transactions among
Non-Sterling, Non-Dollar Countries, 1954

To	From Members of Transferable Accounts Area and EPU 1	Members of Transferable Accounts Area but not EPU 2	Members of Bilateral Group and EPU 3	Members of Bilateral Group but not EPU 4
Members of Transferable Accounts Area and EPU	Yes	Yes	Yes	No
Members of Transferable Accounts Area but *not* EPU	Yes	Yes	No	No
Members of Bilateral Group and EPU	Yes	No	Yes	No
Members of Bilateral Group but *not* EPU	No	No	No	No

Key to membership of each group:

1 Austria, Denmark, German Federal Republic, Greece, Italian Monetary Area, Netherlands Monetary Area, Norway, Sweden.
2 Sudan, Chile, Czechoslovakia, Egypt, Ethiopia, Finland, Poland, Spanish Monetary Area, Thailand, U.S.S.R.
3 Belgian Monetary Area, French Franc Area, Portuguese Monetary Area, Switzerland, Turkey.
4 Argentina, Brazil, Bulgaria, China, Hungary, Iran, Israel, Japan, Lebanon, Paraguay, Peru, Rumania, Syria, Tangier, Uruguay, Vatican City, Yugoslavia.

Source: J. R. SARGENT, «*Convertibility*», Oxford Economic Papers 6 [1954], p. 55.

of payments relating to the *currencies and types of transaction concerned under the new circumstances.* The «new circumstances» are, on the one hand, that the currency restrictions are now eliminated and that «free» demand and supply should be estimated; on the other hand, they imply certain shifts in transactions likely to occur as a consequence of convertibility. These consequences may even lead to the re-imposition of certain trade restrictions if it is felt that, otherwise, demand for foreign currency might rise too much.

5.4 – The concepts just mentioned may be made somewhat more specific by considering in more detail the balance of payments of the country concerned. The items of that balance may be subdivided according to two criteria simultaneously, namely, according to whether they refer to S countries with which there is a surplus or D countries with which there is a deficit, and whether they refer to C countries with which convertibility is to be restored or to N countries with which it is not to be restored. It will be assumed that the type of convertibility envisaged is to make the country's money convertible into *currencies themselves already convertible into gold* [called «convertible money»]. This is not the only type of convertibility conceivable. Let the net transactions with the four groups be as indicated in the table below, where a and c therefore represent surpluses and b and d deficits:

Net transactions [before convertibility]

with countries	*S[urplus]*	*D[eficit]*
C[onvertible]	$+ a$	$- b$
N[on-convertible]	$+ c$	$- d$

Before convertibility, the country considered receives a in convertible money [say dollars, for convenience sake] and c in non-convertible [say soft] money, i.e. in money not yet convertible into dollars. After convertibility, the country will again receive a in dollars and c in soft money. Before convertibility, it paid b in dollars and d in soft money; after convertibility, it will have to pay, as a maximum, both in dollars. This prime disadvantage is the very crux of the matter: an amount d may now have to be paid in dollars. The smaller group N is, the smaller is this disadvantage, i.e. the larger the group of countries which, together with the country considered, also plan to make their currency convertible. Therefore, in a way, the condition to be fulfilled is that the country can supply an extra amount of *d* in dollars.

However, there are other consequences to be taken into account. The country's own currency, say guilders, will be in higher demand as a consequence of the considered convertibility. This means that there will be a tendency for foreign countries to supply more commodities at a somewhat lower price and to demand somewhat fewer products. This will change the balance of payments, be it in an unknown direction. In addition, and partly in response to the tendency just described, there will develop a tendency for the country studied to introduce further restrictions to trade with *N* countries, since this will reduce the obligation to supply dollars to those countries.

5.5 – The above analysis may have indicated how to judge the conditions that have to be fulfilled in order to warrant persistency. It will also be clear that the risks involved in complete convertibility, i.e. including capital items, are far larger than those involved in convertibility on current items alone. It is especially difficult to foresee the switches the public may desire to make in its capital assets. Some of these risks have been demonstrated by the attempt, in 1947, to make sterling convertible. The attempt was unsuccessful and had to be discontinued because of excessive drains on the gold stock of the Sterling Area.

Our final point with regard to convertibility is that the decisions taken by different countries should be *consistent* one with the other: convertibility of currency A into currency B and of B into C has to imply convertibility of A into C also. There have to be groups of mutually convertible currencies and these should be of about equal strength.

5.6 – Since it is clear that universal convertibility, which is a great advantage for international trade, is only possible if a *balance of payments equilibrium* exists, we will now consider somewhat more closely the conditions for such an equillibrium and the instruments that may be used to attain or to maintain it. Balance of payments equilibrium is the financial expression of an equilibrium in the «real» economic sphere, i.e. in production and trade.

We will discuss, in succession, the *general characteristics* of an equilibrated situation and the *possibilities,* in concrete situations, of *attaining and maintaining equilibrium.*

Equilibrium in the balance of payments of any country is *equivalent to equality between total income and total expenditure.* This equivalence is most easily understood as a consequence of the definition of the income of a national economy. In order to obtain a clear picture of the situation we have to specify the nature of the economy; but our conclusion will not depend on that nature. We will assume that imports are only imports of raw materials and semi-finished articles; in a way this is always correct, since it may be maintained that practically no article at the moment of importation is finished in the economic sense of the word: it almost always has to pass some stage of trade, at least. This assumption means that the nation's expenditure [i.e. its spending of income] only consists of expenditure to nationals. Using the following symbols:

Y : the nation's income,
X: total expenditure,
E : exports of goods and services,
M: imports of goods and services,

the definition of income becomes:

$$Y = X + E - M$$

In fact, $X + E$ represents the *value of all production* in its final stage; M represents the costs of the nation's production and, hence, their difference represents income. The phrase «final stage» should be specified, since it may have different meanings; it does not, in our case, mean gross value as far as investment expenditure is concerned. If it did, we would have to deduct depreciation as a separate item, and the definition would then becomes

$$Y = X' + E - N - M$$

where X' is expenditure including gross investments and N is depreciation allowances.

The formula may be written in a different way:

$$X - Y = M - E$$

indicating that the excess, if any, of expenditure over income equals the excess of imports over exports [in the widest sense], or the import surplus. It follows that equality between E and M implies equality between Y and X, or, as it will be called, *spending equilibrium*. In the absence of spending equilibrium, the figure $X - Y$ will be called the *inflationary gap*, if it is positive; if it is negative, the positive figure $Y - X$ will be called the *deflationary gap*.

An important gap between Y and X can only exist for countries with a considerable portion of foreign trade. In a closed economy [and hence for the world as a whole], Y will always, by its definition, be equal to X, since X has to be spent completely inside the country and an increase in X will therefore result in an increase in Y. The criterion for spending equilibrium just given is, therefore, less practical for big countries; one would have to be very precise about the time lag between Y and X in order to apply it correctly. What should be compared is the value of X with the value of Y immediately preceding it; if one compared simultaneous values of X and Y they would always be equal. If the volume of production cannot adapt itself to X, the price level will do the rest of the adapting. Therefore, for a big country a more practical criterion would be the *constancy of prices,* which in its turn would be an inaccurate criterion for small countries: the latter cannot influence the price level much and will never raise prices even if X greatly exceeds Y[1].

This equivalence between balance of payments equilibrium and spending equilibrium for small countries is very important since most countries are, in this sense, small. It implies that one certain way of attaining balance of payments equilibrium is to make national expenditure equal to national income or «to live within the limits set by income». One should, nevertheless, be careful in using this formula; changes in expenditure very often cause changes in income and an attempt to cut expenditure may not always have the expected effect. We will come back to this point below. It is sufficient, for the moment, to say that a country can regulate the *autonomous part of its expenditure,* not the part which depends on its income.

In addition, there is the other characteristic of equilibrium which

---

1. A situation satisfying a criterion of this kind – choosing the price level as its target variable – will be called *monetary equilibrium.*

matters, namely, the *level of production* and hence of employment to which it corresponds. Equilibrium in the wider sense implies a volume of production in which no productive agents are left unused, or where there is only a small idle portion which may be necessary as a reserve for effectuating shifts. This is especially desirable for labour and is equivalent to «*high and stable employment*». Since a higher level of imports accompanies a higher level of production, the latter requires higher exports in order to maintain equilibrium in the balance of payments. Thus, a further condition of high-level equilibrium is that prices be low enough to make exports saleable. Therefore, prices form the second important factor, side by side with national expenditure, whose level has to meet certain conditions if equilibrium at a high level is to be realised.

Countries in which spending equilibrium does not exist and cannot at once be attained will often apply *exchange regulations* of a differentiated type, implying the application of *multiple exchange rates* [cf. section 4.1]. By this means the pressure on the imports of prime necessities is reduced in comparison with the pressure on luxury imports. It has been argued that multiple exchange rates represent a bad instrument of economic policy. The same results can be obtained at less cost to the nation, so the argument runs, under a regime of uniform exchange rates, possibly by better tax policies. In this sense, multiple exchange rates are a second-best solution. It should not be overlooked, however, that better tax policies are not always within the power of the governments considered, for various sociological reasons.

5.7 – It should be realized that the position of equilibrium, as specified in the previous section, is one of *equilibrium relative to other countries*. For the total set of countries to be in equilibrium, they all have to satisfy the conditions indicated: namely, that their balance of payments be in equilibrium and that their price level be «in line with the world market». Now, if we have a «world» of say ten countries, there are ten balance of payments surpluses [positive or negative], but of these only nine are independent of each other. The tenth must always add up with the nine others to zero since, by definition, there cannot be a surplus or deficit for the world as a whole. Therefore, all the ten figures for the autonomous expenditure of the ten countries are not relevant to what will happen to the balances of payments.

It is only their relative level which matters: nine relative figures determine the nine balance of payments gaps. They may, in addition, «blow up» their absolute expenditure without affecting their balances of payments. This «blowing-up» will lead, for the world as a whole, to higher levels of production, as long as there are idle resources, and to higher absolute prices, if full employment has been reached. If the latter phase were attained it could be said that there was «inflation» in the world at large – as in war time – without any balances of payments being in disequilibrium or more in disequilibrium than before.

Furthermore the price levels may be kept «in line» with each other and nevertheless all may rise. In such a process small countries can only, more or less, follow the others; a «world inflation» can only be avoided by concerted action or possibly by the action of some of the large countries.

It also follows that a disruption of equilibrium in a small country may be «due» either to the country's own policy or to the policy of *«imported» inflation* and *«exported» inflation*. By the former term we mean the price rise in a small country which occurs as a consequence of excessive expenditure elsewhere, causing the import prices of the small country to rise. An exported inflation of a small country is a deficit on that country's balance of payments caused by its own excessive expenditure. The latter may not lead to a price rise [small countries can hardly influence world market prices], especially if the balance of payments deficit can be financed. The small countries have the disadvantage of being exposed to imported inflation without being able to prevent it, but they have the advantage of being able to «export» their own inflation, in this sense, as long as they have reserves or as long as they are granted credits.

5.8 – Having formulated the conditions for balance of payments equilibrium in a general way, we are now going to discuss some possibilities of *adaptation* in case of disruption of equilibrium. The adaptations to be discussed are those in the realm of national expenditure and price policy as distinct from the adjustments in the sphere of the Central Bank discussed in chapter 4. As already indicated, these adaptations take somewhat more time; the quickest may act after a few months and some ultimate consequences may occur only after years. Apart from short-term capital transfers, which have al-

ready been discussed in ch. 4, and apart from long-term capital transfers, which have been discussed in ch. 3 and will be considered as
given for the moment, maintenance of balance of payments equilibrium means *equality in changes of imports and exports* in the widest
sense, i.e. of commodities and services. If disrupted, the equilibrium
will have to be restored by reductions or increases in one or both of
these items. The question thus arises as to how such adjustments can
be obtained. The following discussion may be seen as an application
of the general remarks just made on the determinants of the balance
of payments. For both imports and exports, as is true of the transactions in any market, changes may be the consequences of:

[1] *autonomous* changes in demand or supply, without changes in price
    ratios or absolute prices, and
[2] changes in *price ratios,* inducing changes in quantities demanded
    or supplied.

Autonomous changes may be represented on the demand side, i.e.
import side, by reductions in the autonomous expenditure of the
nation. Usually, these are assumed to be certain forms of investment
expenditure and certain forms of public expenditure; in part, they are
also certain forms of expenditure for consumption. Their common
characteristic is their independence of income or prices. If they are
reduced, a reduction in import demand will also result. Autonomous
reductions in imports may also be obtained, to some extent, by the
application of quantitative restrictions [also called quotas]. Their net
extent is not necessarily equal to the direct restrictions applied, since
expenditure may seek other outlets. This is why either an almost
complete system of import quotas or reductions in income will be
needed. If the former policy is not desired, reductions in income will
be the only solution. These can only be obtained by reductions in
autonomous expenditure, which are the determinants of income.

Autonomous changes on the supply side may be effectuated by added
productive capacity, leading to increased supplies of export commodities. In the long run, such changes will be the most satisfactory ones
since they increase rather than restrict production and the standard
of living. In the short run, their influence will be limited since they
require new investments and these are limited to a rather modest
portion of national income.

5.9 – Changes in *price ratios* is the other road towards an adjustment in the balance of payments. The changes may take the form of either:
[i] direct changes in absolute prices of certain commodities, or
[ii] indirect changes, i.e. changes obtained by changes in wage level or rates of exchange.

There are two important sets of problems connected with the application of these changes. First, it may be asked whether they are *necessary at all;* second, whether, if necessary, they *work*. They may not be necessary if the changes in autonomous demand and supply which have caused disequilibrium [or are feared to cause disequilibrium] do themselves restore equilibrium; or if other changes in autonomous demand or supply constitute the normal method for overcoming disequilibrium. There has been much discussion about the first question – whether price changes are necessary at all – in connection with two topics. One was the influence of capital exports or imports on the balances of payments of the countries concerned; the other the influence of reparation payments required from Germany after the First World War. The general reason why, under certain conditions, no price adaptations would be necessary is that the shifts in autonomous demand connected with the transfer discussed would, by themselves, be just sufficient to offset these transfers. Such appears to be the case, upon closer investigation, if the behaviour of a nation is «classical» in the Keynesian sense, i.e. if the nation completely spends an increase in disposible resources. However, if the spending behaviour were Keynesian, i.e. if the complete increase in resources were not spent, a disequilibrium in the balance of payments would remain, which would have to be eliminated in another way.
Even if the shifts in financial resources [which are the origin of a disequilibrium] have not, by themselves, already brought about the adaptation in demand, it may be judged that they will do so in the long run or that the most natural return to equilibrium will be another change in autonomous demand or supply, as discussed earlier.
But there are circumstances under which autonomous changes cannot be hoped for or would have undesirable consequences for, say, the volume of employment. In such circumstances the second issue becomes relevant: namely, whether changes in price ratios, i.e. in the ratios between national and international prices, will be able to do

the job. The answer depends on the reaction of imports and exports to such changes.

5.10 – The total *influence of a change in price ratios* on the balance of payments consists of three components: [i] a change in the volume of imports; [ii] a change in the volume of exports; [iii] a change in the terms of trade. A fall in national prices in relation to foreign ones will raise the volume of exports and so influence the balance of payments favourably. Its influence on the volume of imports is composed of two opposite effects: the rise in export volume will also raise the volume of imports; but the price change will tend to reduce it. The outcome depends on various elasticities. Finally, the influence of the terms of trade on the balance of payments will be unfavourable. Since the different partial effects involved are of opposite signs, the total effect may be negative, zero or positive. If it is negative, zero or slightly positive, it will be insufficient. The case where it is exactly zero is called the case of «*critical elasticities*»; [under certain further assumptions] this is the situation if the sum total of the price elasticities of exports and imports equals one. Therefore, if the elasticities happen to be in this neighbourhood, price ratio changes cannot help to restore payments equilibrium. Even if they are considerably higher, the response of the balance of payments to changes in price ratios that are within the realm of practical possibility may be insufficient. In this case, *quantitative restrictions* offer the only issue from balance of payments difficulties.

The elasticities to which this applies are rather low. There is some evidence that such elasticities actually exist, although opinions among statisticians diverge rather widely. However, there is considerable evidence that, in the long run, elasticities will be considerably higher. It may be, therefore, that the critical situation only applies [or nearly applies] to short-term reactions. This would mean that quantitative restrictions would only be needed as a temporary device and could, afterwards, be removed.

Even if changes in price ratios have the desired effect as far as elasticities of demand and supply are concerned, another problem may arise. How can we obtain such changes? Direct changes in absolute prices of export products cannot be effected by governments in a free economy. If only indirect influencing of these prices is considered feasible, the question arises as to whether the available instruments, i.e. *wage changes* and *changes in exchange rates,* will have the desired effect. Situations may also occur, where insufficient response is obtained, since there are other consequences to be expected in addition to those aimed at. A wage change cannot exceed a certain limit and may, for that reason, be insufficient. A change in the rate of exchange will have consequences for the internal price and wage level. Whether the net effect is sufficient depends on the extent of these consequences. Statistical investigations have shown, in this case also, that under boom conditions changes in exchange rates do not alter the ratios of national to foreign prices. Here again, quantitative restrictions are the only solution. Therefore, the two cases where either elasticities are low or price changes cannot be large enough represent cases in which such restrictions are justified. This was the basis of what was called the British «austerity policy» under the Labour Government after the Second World War.

PART II – INTERNATIONAL ECONOMIC INTEGRATION

6 – TARGETS AND INSTRUMENTS OF INTERNATIONAL ECONOMIC INTEGRATION

6.1 – In the preceding five chapters we have dealt with the essence of international economic relations between autonomous nations. We have also tried to clarify the mechanism of these relations by discussing certain possible ways in which they can be affected. Thus, after having indicated the possibilities of regulating them, we shall now discuss how far we want to regulate these relations. Such regulation, when aimed at more systematically, is nowadays usually called *«integration»* of the various national economies. Integration may be said to be the creation of the most desirable structure of the international economy, removing artificial hindrances to its optimum operation and deliberately introducing all the desirable elements of co-ordination or unification. The problem of integration, therefore, forms part of a more general problem, namely, that of the *optimum economic policy*. When making recommendations on economic policy we are actually leaving the sphere of objective science – or at least introducing outside elements. Since, nevertheless, a good deal of economic analysis will have to be used we will warn the reader every time such extra-economic elements are being used.

6.2 – It will be useful to make some *general remarks* on the subject of *economic policy* before embarking upon our special case of integration. Economic policy will be taken to mean the activity of public authorities, as such, in the economic field. It therefore excludes the activity of public authorities as producers or consumers, as far as the normal aims of production and consumption are concerned. As soon as more general aims are involved, policy begins. There are greatly differing types of policy, however. An initial distinction may be made between *qualitative* and *quantitative* policy. By an act of qualitative economic policy we mean every change in the organization or structure of society, as far as it is of economic importance. By acts of quantitative economic policy we mean changes in the data controlled by public authorities within an unchanged framework of organization. Examples of changes in organization may be the introduction of a monopoly by law, the dissolution of a monopoly, changes in property rights or the introduction of a new international agency. Examples of changes in data within a given organization are changes in tax rates, in public expenditure or in the rate of discount of the Central Bank. Data partly under the control of public authorities, as in the cases just quoted, will be called *instruments* or instrument variables. The other data, such as weather conditions, population growth, or technical development, are not under the control of public authorities.

Some of the most frequently used instruments have already been mentioned: taxes, public expenditure and the rate of discount. They could be specified further and others could be added. A number of examples will be given below.

There are wide differences in the scope and extent of either type of policy: both may be far-reaching or modest in scope. Fundamental qualitative policies may be called *reforms* or even *revolutions* if they change the structure of society in important points; but there may also be modest changes in organization, such as the introduction of collective bargaining or the establishment of a new tax. Quantitative policies also may be far-reaching or modest. In a depression very important public expenditure may be added or tax reductions applied; in a situation near monetary equilibrium only slight changes in some tax rates may be considered. Quantitative policy in a country with extensive government intervention may use a large number of instruments, e.g. rationing applied to a large number of commodities, detailed price regulations and so on. Quantitative policy in a laissez-faire country may have a very limited number of taxes to manipulate.

The fundamental problem of qualitative economic policy is to find the «optimum order», that is, a set of institutions which maximizes national or social well-being. We will not discuss this problem in this book but take it for granted that a «mixed» system having both a public and a private sector is close to the optimum[1].

In the field of quantitative policies a distinction can be made between *direct* and *indirect intervention;* the former being the direct interference

---

1. Cf. J. Tinbergen, «*The Theory of the Optimum Regime*», in Selected Papers, Amsterdam, 1959.

with market forces such as rationing and price-fixing. Important instruments, from the international point of view, are the ones directly affecting foreign trade: import duties, quantitative restrictions on imports, or currency regulations. Indirect intervention operates above all through *financial policy* [credit as well as fiscal policy]. It goes without saying that the introduction of some new type of intervention represents an act of qualitative policy; once it exists, however, the changes in rations, prices, etc., are only of a quantitative character. As always, there may be borderline cases.

6.3 – An important aspect of acts of qualitative policy is the choice between *centralization* and *decentralization* or, rather, the choice of the degree of centralization.

This choice has to be made in terms of both national and international economic policy. Within each country certain functions of economic life will be performed more efficiently when organized centrally while others are better decentralized. The same problem is to be seen in private business and in extra-economic – political, cultural and social– activities. Centralization or decentralization may be defined in the *geographical* sense as wel as in the *functional* sense: certain activities may be left to local authorities – which would be an example of geographical decentralization – or to specialized private organs, each of them national, but performing only restricted types of functions. In a way, the question of the most desirable economic policy – particularly as far as intervention by public authorities is concerned – may be said to be identical to the question of what degree of decentralization in economic activities is most healthy. Private enterprise is an example of decentralization.

The main topic of this part of the present book – international economic integration – is intimately connected with the question of decentralization and centralization. The question that will have to be answered is precisely this: Which functions in international economic life should be subject to centralized control and which should be left to individual countries, enterprises or persons?

Some general remarks may be made and *formal directives* given even before the aim of economic policy is specified.

Since economic policy means the handling of instruments by policy-makers, it seems natural that the degree of centralization wanted

59

should, to a large extent, depend on the nature of its effect on the well-being of each of the countries concerned. Classified according to their effects, instruments may be of four types. If a certain change in an instrument acts in the same direction on the well-being of all countries concerned, it will be called *supporting,* since the use of such an instrument by one country will support the policies of the other countries. If a change in an instrument used by country A acts in opposite directions inside and outside that country, the instrument will be called *conflicting:* its use by country A conflicts with the objectives of other countries' policies. If the instrument does not affect at all the well-being of other countries, we will call it *neutral.* Finally, there will be instruments that act in a mixed way; these wil be called *mixed* instruments.

An example of a supporting instrument is the level of government expenditure in a general depression or in the case of general inflation: in both cases the effect will be parallel for all countries concerned. In times of depression, an increase in government expenditure in any country will act favourably on all countries. In times of inflation, a decrease in public expenditure in one country will be wholesome for the other countries as well. An example of a conflicting instrument, in the case of a general depression, is the rate of exchange of any one country. A reduction in this rate will affect the country itself favourably, but the other countries, as a rule, unfavourably. Examples of neutral instruments will be instruments of only a local character. The effects of most instruments will depend on circumstances; this is why the distinction made is only formal. The instrument of government expenditure will act in a mixed way, for instance, if certain countries are in an inflationary situation and others in a deflationary situation.

In general, there is a strong case for decentralization since it means freedom to groups or individuals, which constitutes an element of direct satisfaction. In addition, it may avoid costs.

6.4 – Apart from this general argument in favour of decentralization, there will be arguments in favour of centralization. These primarily apply to the first two types of instrument, since the other countries have a strong interest in their use. This interest is parallel in the case of supporting instruments and opposed in the case of conflicting instruments. Therefore, the aims of centralization in these two cases will be different: centralized decisions on supporting instruments will tend to *intensify* their use, whereas centralized use of conflicting instruments will tend to *eliminate* or *mitigate* their use. The disadvantages of centralization will only be compensated by important advantages if the character of the instruments under discussion is of an unambiguous supporting or of a clearly conflicting character.

In less clear-cut cases, i.e. in any case where the instrument is neutral and often where it has mixed consequences, there is more to be said in favour of decentralization.

6.5 – The *choice of the instruments* of economic policy has to be made dependent on a number of circumstances. It goes without saying that the nature of the problems to be solved will have to be taken into account. This is particularly true of the extent of the problems. The same problem, when it presents itself in a modest size, may be solvable with modest means; but when it is of greater extent it may require more fundamental acts. War-time disturbances and similar emergency situations usually require more direct interventions than smaller and more temporary disturbances. During and after the latter, sufficient help may be expected from the automatic reactions of economic life. A short supply in only one crop will be followed by a price rise which automatically diverts demand to other products and so solves the difficulty. A general shortage of food cannot be remedied in this way since a general price rise will not divert demand sufficiently.

Apart from the nature and the extent of the problems to be solved by any form of economic policy, the choice of instruments will depend on certain *pre-conceived ideas* the extreme examples of which are *complete regulation* on the one hand and *complete absence of it* on the other hand. These ideas cannot in themselves be divorced from the aims of economic policy, to be discussed below. Historically, it may be said that the tendency towards freedom was greatest when political power was in the hands of business leaders and that the tendency towards complete regulation exists with military and with communist groups as leading politicians. It cannot be denied that greater emphasis on the interests of the masses sometimes requires more intervention; but it is also probable that the necessity for intervention tends to be over-emphasized by those anxious to exert power for its own sake and as a reaction to a lack of power in the past. It is the serious task of economics and sociology to try to find, as often as possible, objective criteria for the choice of instruments. Some attempts in this direction will be found in this text.

6.6 – The relevance of any act of economic policy depends on the *targets* or *aims* set. The choice of these aims or *objectives of economic policy* is itself extra-economic, just as the aim of each individual in economic matters cannot be explained by economic reasoning but has to be considered as given. Whereas, however, the objectives one man aims at may, as a rule, be left to himself so long as he does not definitely interfere with the interests of others, the setting of aims for the economic policy of a community of different individuals involves difficult problems. A well-known formula for the goal to be aimed at is the pursuance of «*maximum welfare*» for the community or the furtherance of the «*general interest*»; but upon closer consideration these formulae are «empty phrases» unless further specified.

Human welfare is affected by different elements, the most important of which, from the economic point of view, appear to be:

[a] those referring to *individual well-being*, namely the availability of goods and of leisure, and

[b] those referring to man's *relations to other individuals*, namely freedom, justice and peace.

These are solemn words but the reader is asked to excuse them and consider them as a very brief indication of some of the most important complexes of the relevant elements. Moreover, the list is not exhaustive, and the valuation of the various elements varies in time and differs between individuals. Some individuals sometimes like the opposites of justice and peace.

If individuals could live independently of each other the elements under [b] might not come into play and each could strive for his individual optimum of goods and leisure, under the standard proviso that more goods can only be had if less leisure is taken. Several circumstances, however, make for the mutual dependence of individuals. The mere fact of their mutual proximity introduces the possibility of conflicts and the elements under [b] come into play. This is reinforced very much by the technical possibilities of increasing production opened up by co-operation in the production process. These two forms of dependence make the problem of economic policy extremely complicated, especially because of the inequality in individual capacities and tastes. They destroy the possibility for each individual to strive for his own optimum. Common decisions have to be taken and the decisions one individual would prefer differ from those desired by others. They differ because of varying tastes, differences in insight and wisdom and plain divergence of interests. So far, no generally accepted method has been found to reconcile these differences. To be specific and to give an important example, no method is available to decide whether a transfer of one dollar from Mr A to Mr B means an increase or a decrease in welfare. It is much more difficult to say whether a transfer of $ 1 milliard from country A to country B implies an increase in general welfare or not. Still more difficult are choices between more or fewer regulations [which may increase justice but will decrease freedom] or between an armed struggle and its avoidance [the struggle may bring greater justice but it interrupts peace]. Unfortunately, even international peace in the nuclear era seems to have a restricted value to certain governments.

At this stage of our knowledge and insight an accurate and generally acceptable formulation is only possible for a few aims of economic policy, whereas other aims cannot be so formulated. A relatively high degree of agreement exists about the «*aims of high production*», i.e. the aims [1] of using all productive resources, and [2] of using them in the most efficient way, since the interests of individuals in this respect are largely parallel. Difficulties arise as soon as questions of distribution are considered, because of differences as to the interpretation of justice. Only to the extent that distribution indirectly affects efficiency, do more possibilities of agreement arise.

Difficulties also arise as to the *choice of the instruments of economic policy,* the main dilemma then being the one between freedom, on the one hand, and the aims [1] and [2], with justice, on the other hand.

Agreement on these aims is only possible in very clear-cut cases, e.g. on measures towards a more equal distribution if the existing inequality is very marked, and agreement on the use of instruments of detailed intervention is only possible if very strong disequilibria are threatening society.

Briefly, therefore, the main groups of aims of economic policy may be formulated in the following way:

[1] the use of all *productive resources,* implying the *avoidance of* instability in production,

[2] the use of these resources in the *most efficient* way,

[3] a more *equal distribution* of incomes between persons and between countries in so far as there is marked inequality, and

[4] the use of *instruments of detailed intervention only in order to prevent strong disequilibria.*

Using the above argument even this formulation contains concepts that are only vaguely defined. At best, it could be added that what is understood by «marked inequality» and «strong disequilibrium» depends on the development of public opinion and will, as a rule, be defined by political decisions in the more general sense.

Notwithstanding this restricted set of more or less accepted aims, it is remarkable that a relatively well-defined set of rules of economic policy can be derived. This is due to the fact that economic life is continually threatened by disruptions of equilibrium due to variations in crops, new inventions and political events and that the skilful maintenance of equilibrium is already a complicated art of considerable importance to general well-being. In addition, the inherent tendency towards great inequalities is so clear that permanent redistribution with a minimum loss of efficiency is the other main technique required.

6.7 – If it is true that a certain consensus of opinion prevails with regard to the general aims formulated above, it cannot be denied that the big differences in economic policies between the non-communist and the communist countries [already referred to in section 6.5] can only partly be explained in this way. It is true that inequalities in the latter countries were larger than in many western countries and it is true that the disturbances created by the First World War in Russia and by the Second World War in the present communist countries were large indeed. But there are other countries where this also applies and these countries are not – or, shall we say, not yet – communist. Certain differences in history, in national character and in political aspirations – and some pure coincidences – have also to be accepted as part of the explanation.

The fact of the existence of the two political blocks, unfortunately, has to be considered largely a datum in present-day problems of economic policy. The time when it could have been avoided by a wiser economic policy [in the widest sense] seems to have passed, although there are some indications of lessening differences between the systems as welfare grows. There are, thus, wide divergences in basic economic organization. This also necessarily affects international relations. Centrally organized, or at least highly interventionist, countries will also have centrally organized or highly regulated international relations. Similarly, less strongly organized countries will prefer less organized international relations. In their intercourse with the first group they will be forced, nevertheless, to organize contacts to some extent, if only to create the «opposite numbers» to the civil servants of the centralized countries for the necessary discussions, negotiations and executive measures. They may, on the other hand, introduce decentralized elements in the executive sphere inside their own countries to the extent that they think is desirable. In other words, international relations between countries of different political structures will necessarily have to be dependent on these national structures and, in a way, represent some intermediate form. The more decentralized countries cannot freely choose their relations with centralized countries. These relations will not be discussed to any great extent in this book, since political elements will be much more decisive in the next few years than will economic factors.

International relations between the more decentralized countries themselves can, however, be shaped more deliberately and, therefore, according to the principles commonly adhered to by these countries. We are going to deal mainly with these relations in the following chapters.

6.8 – Turning now to the problem of *integration* as a special aspect of international economic policy, we are going to discuss this according to the groups of instruments of economic policy. We distinguish two main groups, namely those commonly considered as *national instruments* and those seen as *international ones*. The latter are the instruments directly affecting international transactions; all the others will be grouped into the former category. By so doing, we are paying lip-service to tradition rather than applying a thorough analysis, since the very problem is exactly to what extent national instruments should remain sovereign national instruments. In chapter 7 national economic policies will be considered in their relation to integration; the instruments considered are mainly the indirect ones of financial policy and the instruments determining the general price level. As a subsidiary group, certain specified taxes will be considered. In chapter 8 the non-monetary instruments and in chapter 9 the monetary instruments directly affecting international transactions will be discussed.

Chapter 10 deals with the integration of development and, in a concluding chapter, the agencies of international economic co-operation will be very briefly discussed.

7 – MINIMUM CONDITIONS FOR INTEGRATION

7.1 – Economic integration of a number of countries consists of the centralization, at a supra-national level, of a number of instruments of economic policy, preferably of those instruments showing considerable external effects [conflicting or supporting]. Centralization is an act which may take various forms, weaker and stronger ones. Accordingly, we may distinguish between different forms of integration, depending on the strength of the centralization chosen. The weakest form of centralization is the one where governments remain completely autonomous but *consult* each other before taking measures with regard to the instruments under discussion. A stronger form of centralization consists of consultation followed by some agreement, a form which we may call *co-ordination*. In both cases centralization is not only weak but also incidental. Again, a stronger form may be an *agreement of a lasting character* limiting the use of some instruments of economic policy. Evidently the strongest form of centralization is obtained by the establishment of *one supra-national authority;* this form implies a unified process of policy-making.

7.2 – In the case of optimum integration not necessarily every instrument of economic policy will be used in a centralized way. On the contrary, instruments of an almost neutral character will be left in the hands of lower authorities, depending on the area within which neutrality prevails. In principle, there may exist several levels of policy-makers, such as local, provincial [or departmental], national and supra-national, each of them handling a set of instruments. The central government of an integrated area will deal with the instruments requiring centralized use. Such an arrangement is better than co-ordination only, since simple co-ordination does not guarantee a proper handling of the instruments requiring centralized use.

Once a central [supra-national] authority has been created there is a probability that it will deal with its instruments of policy in a *uni-*

form way for the whole area. Thus, there may develop a tendency to unify social insurance schemes or taxes even if this is not strictly necessary for the proper operation of the area's economy. Social insurance contributions need not be uniform since wages and labour conditions need not be. The only condition which must be fulfilled here is that the total labour remuneration must be proportional to the marginal productivity of labour in the various countries, but it goes without saying that uniform contributions may somewhat reduce the costs of social insurance.

Similarly, there is no necessity for the general indirect tax rates to be uniform. If France, to quote an example, has higher indirect taxes than Germany, the exchange rate of the French franc may compensate for this difference without distorting the mechanism of competition.

7.3 – From the two examples just quoted we see that *uniformity is not always necessary;* but it may mean a simplification and hence a cost reduction of administration. Uniformity or co-ordination is not necessary for a number of instruments of an almost neutral character. Measures affecting only small areas, such as local communities, can be left to the corresponding authorities. This applies to the regulation of local markets and the taxes affecting them – say, the market for residential building or for various types of services, including theatres, local transportation, and so on. There is also a group of instruments which may be handled by the national governments. Direct taxes can be fixed by these governments; within certain limits deviations will not disturb the proper operation of the economic process, since, as a first approximation, direct taxes do not affect marginal producers.

7.4 – *Uniformity is required,* however, for the instruments of a non-neutral character. An important example is represented by the differences in indirect tax rates between various commodities. Some more examples will be discussed below. The point to be made here is that certain minimum conditions must be met in order that a group of countries can be integrated. If the instruments of a *supporting* or a *conflicting* nature are not uniform, then integration will lead to the disruption of some fundamental equilibria. Whether instruments have one of these characteristics depends, as we know, on the influence they exert on other countries' welfare. Of the main instruments of internal economic policy mentioned in chapter 6, those that influence the general level of activity will also influence other countries' welfare to a considerable extent. Instruments influencing the distribution of income between groups or individuals will make themselves felt to a much lesser degree in foreign countries. These will not, as a rule, so much affect total imports or even imports from individual countries.

The aim of influencing the general level of activity will usually be formulated in the wording: *maintenance of balance of payments equilibrium at a high level of employment.* To maintain the balance of payments equilibrium is equivalent [as we saw in chapter 5] to the maintenance of balance between total income and total expenditure, or, again, to the avoidance of the use of «inflationary financing» for the country as a whole, i.e. for the total private and public income and expenditure. The exact meaning of the term «inflationary financing» will be discussed below. In principle, however, such an equilibrium is possible [as we also stated in chapter 5] at different levels of employment. Maintaining the balance of payments equilibrium at a low level of employment would mean maintaining stagnation and fixing the demand for imports as well as the domestic demand at a lower level than is possible with the country's resources. This is why the second part of the aim was formulated as the maintenance of the balance of payments equilibrium at a high-employment level.

Therefore, while the use of inflation as a permanent instrument of economic policy is undesirable, attaining high employment from an initial position of low employment may require the temporary use of credit creation. It should also be kept in mind that a regular increase of the money supply of a country in order to meet the increased demand for liquidity at constant prices does not mean inflation in this context. Inflation, according to the definition adhered to here, would be the creation of more money than is needed for financing high-employment production at the desired price level plus financing increased liquidity holdings.

It is not always easy to avoid, at least temporarily, the use of inflationary financing. It may happen that in a period of «high liquidity preference» [i.e. when people want to hold ample liquid reserves] more money is needed to maintain high and stable employment than in a subsequent period of lower liquidity preference. The presence of ample cash reserves may induce people, once they no longer prefer to hold reserves to that extent, to spend more than their current income and so to cause a boom and inflationary price rises. Under such circumstances taxes should be increased or attractive loans made in order to «drain» circulation. The policy of high and stable employment is, therefore, to watch not only income flows but also the composition and use made of assets.

7.5 – There are *two groups* of *main instruments* for this policy and a number of *subsidiary* ones. The first main group is that of financial policy, consisting of public expenditure policy and tax policy. By an appropriate manipulation of these instruments total internal demand can be kept at the desired level and its composition may be made optimum.

The level of demand may be influenced by public expenditure as well as by taxes. If a decline in private demand occurs, e.g. as a consequence of decreased investments, public demand may be increased by higher expenditure. In addition, an attempt can be made to stimulate private expenditure by lowering taxes. Therefore, it may depend on the *composition of total national expenditure* that is desired whether more emphasis should be laid on one instrument or the other. If important public investment projects are available, the first line may be followed. If, however, there are only projects of low priority, to stimulate private demand may be a better use of the country's resources.

Once a tax reduction is preferred to increase public expenditure, a further question arises as to *which taxes* should be reduced. The first choice may be between direct and indirect taxes. Lower *indirect* taxes will probably influence consumption more than an equal change in direct taxes. If more consumption is considered desirable, there may, therefore, be a case for decreasing indirect taxes. Even investment may be stimulated in this case, if lack of sales – rather than lack of financial means – has kept it down. If, on the other hand, private investment was low because of a lack of finance, a reduction in *direct* taxes may be more appropriate. In times of depression, a reduction in direct taxes might, however, lead to increased hoarding rather than to increased expenditure and then it would be less efficient as an instrument of economic policy.

After a decision has been taken as to the general category of taxes that should be lowered, another choice has to be made as to precisely which of the individual taxes to choose. We will come back to this question when we discuss the situation in individual industries.

7.6 – First, we will discuss the *second group of main instruments* of internal economic policy. They refer to the general level of *prices, wages* and *other income rates*. This group of economic variables will not, as a rule, be considered to be instruments in the proper sense, since they are not «data». Certain components of these variables are data, however; and, sometimes, there may be direct government control of prices as well as of wage rates or land rents. A general method of influencing them is to change the *rate of exchange;* this is probably the most powerful instrument, but an instrument that can only be used occasionally. In addition, this instrument can hardly be said to be an internal instrument.

Whatever the precise instrument chosen, the main point to be made here is, again, that the regulation of the general price level of a country is an important, and, in fact, indispensable, element of a country's economic policy. Its economic function is the *regulation,* or adjustment, *of the country's competitive power*. The necessity of making adjustments may appear from time to time in a country's general development. If a country can only maintain high and stable employment by permanent inflation this is an indication of the necessity of adjusting its competitive power. Of course, a better solution would be a general increase in its productivity; but this cannot, as a rule, be obtained within a short period. There may therefore be no other solution than a devaluation or a general reduction in prices and income rates.

The necessity of employing this difficult complex of instruments will vary directly with the size and frequency of fluctuations in prices in the world's leading countries. Therefore, the importance of a policy of stable prices in those countries will be clear [cf. ch. 8].

7.7 – It may be hoped that an appropriate use of the two groups of main instruments – financial policy and price policy in the above sense – will, as a rule, lead to a fairly stable development of national income as a whole. An appropriate use presupposes, however, one important condition. *Business men should have and should show understanding for this policy.* They ought not to be alarmed by temporary increases in government activity meant to compensate for their own decreased activity. They seemed to be alarmed in the thirties, especially in the United States, and consequently became reluctant to start investment activity after the 1932 turning point. Because of this reluctance, they undermined government policy and, indirectly, national well-being. By such an attitude – if continued *ad absurdum* – any policy, even the best one, may be undermined; it is not constructive. Fortunately, there have been profound changes for the good in the understanding shown by business for this type of economic policy.

7.8 – As already observed, the instruments affecting the general level of activity are also likely to influence other countries' well-being, either in the same direction or in the opposite direction, as well as that of the country considered. In the terms previously used, they will either be supporting or conflicting instruments and, for that reason, their decentralized use would probably lead to deviations from an international optimum situation. In periods of depression an increase in expenditure or a decrease in taxes is not only in the interest of the country itself, but also of the other countries. The country concerned might, therefore, underestimate the advantages and apply the instrument to a lesser degree than desirable. Or, to put it in other terms, *concerted action* may lead to better results than unco-ordinated action. The risks for the individual country [i.e. that by an isolated application of these instruments it would adversely affect its balance of payments and hence its gold reserve] may keep such a country from taking action if there is no concerted action. Similar conclusions may be drawn for the opposite case of general inflation where the interest of all countries lies in concerted action to decrease expenditure.

While expenditure and tax receipts are examples of supporting instruments of national economic policy, manipulations of the general price level – either by wage policy or by a policy of changing exchange rates – are of the conflicting type. Lowering the general price level will, as a rule, bring competitive advantages to the country that adopts such a course, at the expense of other countries. Or, in well-known terms, this represents a «beggar-my-neighbour» policy. Thus, there is sometimes a danger of a «competition in devaluation», as in

72

the 1930's. For these reasons, these instruments should also be subject to international supervision in some form or another [cf. ch. 9].

Using our own terminology from chapter 6, there is scope, therefore, for more or less *centralizing the use of the instruments just discussed,* with a view to intensifying the use of supporting and reducing the use of conflicting instruments. When applying this device, we should, however, keep in mind that the character of the same instruments may vary according to circumstances. If there is not a general depression, but the depression is confined to a few countries, it may be wise to increase expenditure in the depressed group and to decrease it elsewhere. Even if, generally speaking, we wanted to reduce the use of devaluation as a policy, there might be circumstances in which some country simply has to devalue.

While advocating a certain central control of the instruments just discussed, we must keep clearly in mind the strong resistance existing against such a control. It should, therefore, be confined to the indispensable minimum required by our analysis. This, it should not be forgotten, is based on the aim of the general well-being of the nations as a group and should be accepted, for that reason, as a strong argument. This indispensable minimum is based on the fact that the relevant elements for other countries' well-being are: [1] the value of the «*inflationary*» or «*deflationary gap*», i.e. the difference between total expenditure and total income rather than the value of each of these two separately and [2] the *general price level* of each country. Therefore, central control should be founded on these two crucial elements and one could leave the choice of the components to the countries themselves. Since the inflationary or deflationary gap of the country as a whole equals the gap in the private sector plus the one in the public sector, and the first will only be under the indirect control of the government, the primary object for central control should be the «gap» in the public sector [cf. ch. 11].

7.9 – Even if a smooth development of national income is warranted, problems may nevertheless remain for *individual industries.* There are continual changes in technology, in tastes and in natural conditions; and, occasionally, these may suddenly threaten some industries. In the long run, this may mean that certain plants will have to vanish and factors of production will have to move to other industries. In the short run, such changes cannot be made without creating grave difficulties. Therefore, there is a need for temporary support for such industries in one form or another. Here the *subsidiary instruments of economic policy* may be useful. These may be *credit policy,* changes in *individual taxes* – to which allusion has already been made – or *temporary subvention.* There may even be the need for *temporary import duties,* if these are more easily organized than alternative measures. In special cases where the price mechanism does not work efficiently, quantitative restrictions on imports or on demand generally, or on supply or, finally, on both, may even be needed. This is especially true if there are sudden disturbances of equilibrium of some magnitude in markets where demand and supply are highly inelastic [agricultural markets].

The instruments now under discussion are intended to change the distribution of activity rather than its general level. Thus, they should be subject to a lesser degree of international supervision. Their influence on other countries' well-being is less pronounced and they, therefore, more closely approach the neutral type of instrument. This point might also be formulated in the following way: relevant to foreign countries and, therefore, ineligible for decentralization is the total surplus or deficit on public account; much less relevant, however, and, hence, appropriate for decentralization is the distribution over the component items. The irrelevance of this distribution for foreign countries is accentuated by the temporary character recommended for these «subsidiary» instruments.

Since it is a well-known tendency, however, for such instruments [i.e. taxes, subsidies or quantitative restrictions applied to specfiic industries] to be used for a longer time than originally intended, it should be emphasized that they should, in any case, not hamper, in the long run, the correct use of productive resources from the international point of view. They should be only *temporary* if, in order to meet a shock, they do hamper such a correct use; and they should, if not conceived of as temporary, obey certain rules to make sure that they do not *violate the international division of labour.* An important example is to be found in the system of indirect taxes operated by most countries. Usually, there exist high taxes [excises] on certain commodities such as tobacco products, alcoholic beverages and some other luxuries. There are provisions, however, to ensure that exports

74

of such products are not taxed to the same extent ; i.e. there are *exemptions* or *drawbacks* which tend to neutralize the tax. At the same time, there are «*compensatory duties*» on the imports of such products, in order to equalize the burdens on foreign importers and home producers. Such provisions do not attempt to falsify the decisions of producers as to what to produce for the international market. The rule should be, indeed, that the tax burden for different products, when exported, should not be different, so as to allow the relative costs of production to reflect the relative actual sacrifices needed to obtain the various products.

8 – THE INTEGRATION OF CURRENT
TRANSACTIONS

8.1 – We are now going to discuss in more detail the measures to be taken in order to arrive at the integration of a number of national economies. The discussion will deal first of all with the integration of *current transactions*. In the later chapters other aspects of integration will be dealt with.

It appears useful to make a distinction between *negative* and *positive* integration. By the former we mean measures consisting of the abolition of a number of impediments to the proper operation of an integrated area. By the latter we mean the creation of new institutions and their instruments or the modification of existing instruments.

Before embarking upon this discussion we wish to remind the reader of the actual processes of integration in the world of today. Several continents show examples of such processes. The oldest examples are those on integration processes already completed, such as the unification of the United States and Germany in the previous century. At present, the integration of the six countries of the European Economic Community [or Common Market] is the most important example. The integration process is based mainly on the Treaty of Rome, concluded in 1957, but also on the treaties underlying the European Coal and Steel Community and Euratom applying to the same countries. A considerable number of countries are «associated» with the Community; these are mostly African countries which formerly were French, Belgian or Italian colonies. Since these countries are under-developed, they need provisions differing from the ones applied to countries with a more developed economy. Association is also possible for more developed countries desiring ultimately to become full members or fully developed countries which cannot be full members for political reasons. Unfortunately, the negotiations between. the United Kingdom and the European Economic Community were broken off by President De Gaulle's intervention early in 1963.

Other examples of integration can be found in Latin America. The countries of Central America are involved in an attempt to create one bigger market. So are the main Latin American countries which decided to establish the Latin American Free Trade Area [LAFTA]. Some beginnings of integration are under discussion in the Arab region and in Central Africa. The Arab League has already reduced the number of trade impediments between its member countries. In South-East Asia, finally, a small number of countries are in the process of integration.

8.2 – *Negative integration* consists primarily of the *reduction of trade impediments* between national economies, that is, the reduction of import duties or the expansion of quotas. As is shown by welfare economics, the situation of maximum welfare is characterized by uniform prices for all commodities coinciding with the prices resulting from free competition. Trade impediments are incompatible with this optimum requirement and their elimination will lead to a *better division of labour* between the producers of the area and hence to increased well-being in the area as a whole. Each country will specialize in the products in which it has the greatest comparative advantages.

This process may cause a change in the industrial pattern; some industries will have to reduce their production, and others will have to increase theirs. This may necessitate the *retraining* of workers if the process is carried out quickly; in a slow transition, retaining may be avoided since only the younger generation will then have to be taught another technique. A similar question arises with regard to the *replacement of capital goods* by other types. A rapid reorientation of production will require additional investments, whereas a slow process will require only the new investments to change their character. Consequently, there exists an *optimum speed of integration*, for which total costs are a minimum; that is, the sum total of [i] the losses on the current production process that has not been reoriented and [ii] the additional retraining costs and additional investments needed.

In the Treaty of Rome a *transition period* of some twelve to fifteen years has been assumed to be desirable; in the meantime, endeavours have been made to shorten the period by the «acceleration» of integration. The Treaty has also created the *European Investment Bank* in order to assist industrialists and workers in the process of reorientation.

8.3 – Certain *exceptions* are generally admitted; agricultural production has, for example, to be maintained to a certain extent for strategic and for social reasons. Infant industries may be protected temporarily; here, a period of five years is usually taken as acceptable. Nevertheless, it may be asked whether import duties should not always be avoided and *subsidies* be applied where protection is considered legitimate. Subsidies, especially a lump sum meant to cover part of an industry's fixed costs, do not affect marginal costs and, hence, do not «falsify» prices. They have the political advantage that their payment has to be a deliberate act and cannot be hidden from the public. Only in cases where the administration of subsidies would be more complicated, and hence more costly, than the administration of duties, may the latter be preferred.

8.4 – The general abolition of import duties by a high-tariff country will affect the competitive position of that country. The general price and wage level of such a country will be higher than that of a low-tariff country. In order to maintain its competitive position, and hence the balance of payments equilibrium, the country has to be permitted to *adjust its exchange rate* accordingly.

8.5 – *Positive integration* or the creation both of new institutions with their instruments and the modification of existing instruments applies, in principle, to the institutions and instruments requiring centralized handling. As a minimum, this refers to measures needed to *avoid a distortion* of the process of free competition. The most important example has already been mentioned in section 7.4; it concerns *indirect taxation*. While there is not much harm in differences of the general level of indirect taxes between member countries, there is in the differences between such taxes for individual commodities. If commodity A is taxed more heavily than commodity B in country I, this should also be so in country II and to the same extent if distortions in the competitive situation are to be avoided. We may formulate this rule by saying that the *relative indirect taxation* of any two countries must be uniform.

8.6 – More generally, positive integration should consist of the creation of all the institutions required by the welfare optimum which have to be handled in a centralized way. Prominent among these is the institution in charge of the redistribution of incomes required by welfare economics, particularly if its purpose is to effectuate a *redistribution of incomes between countries*. The redistribution within countries obviously can be left to the national governments. In a modest way the European Investment Bank may perform this task, but one may wonder whether a bank is the appropriate institution here, since there is also scope for a treasury.

Another example is the *regulation of unstable markets* with a market area surpassing national frontiers. Most of European agricultural policy consists of such market regulations.

A third example is the need for some *planning agency* at the supranational level. The sound preparation of economic policy, at all levels, requires a type of planning corresponding to the degree of intervention. For present-day mixed economies this does not mean a very detailed method of planning, but, nevertheless, it does imply planning a number of the more important sectors of economic life.

The examples of institutions and instruments of positive integration do not refer only to what is needed at the level of an integrated area; they also apply to larger areas. This has already been recognized for the regulation of unstable markets, which is the subject of some world-wide commodity agreements, and for some aspects of income redistribution and planning, taken care of by the International Bank for Reconstruction and Development and the United Nations Secretariat. But even here, there is scope for a more intensive form of application, to be discussed later [ch. 10].

8.7 – A subject for positive integration may also be seen in a *supervision* of the measures taken by member countries for the development of their less developed regions. In some countries *railway rates* have been used as an instrument for this purpose. Such measures, again, should not distort the process of competition; for example, railway rates should reflect the actual costs of transportation. If there is a need to stimulate development, instruments should be used which are directly related to the problem to be solved. Usually, this implies the employment of unemployed; subsidies for this employment are better than artificially low railway rates. In fact, the existence of unemployment in the regions concerned provides an indication that labour costs are too high and subsidies will help to reduce them. Artificially low railway rates will have several consequences, different from the one aimed at, which do not make sense. They stimulate the development not only of the underdeveloped regions but also of the developed regions and will lead to numerous cases of the wrong choice of the location of plants for heavy products.

8.8 – An important question with regard to the integration process concerns the extent of the *changes to be expected in trade, production and well-being*. These problems are not easy to solve. To begin with, the processes involved are complicated; not only will one industry be affected much more than another industry, but even within each industry one product may be affected much more than other products or even qualities of products. Moreover, general statistical information on some of the relevant variables, such as costs of production, is very scanty and vague. Information available to enterprises will be considered confidential and hardly be made available to the public. For all these reasons the number of estimates available are limited and of limited value, but some impressions have been obtained.

A distinction should be made between the effects to be expected in the short as opposed to the long run. In the short run, the reduction of tariffs will lead to changes in consumption patterns without changing the structure of production or the degree of specialization. In a somewhat longer run the latter changes may occur, leading to increases in efficiency and, hence, in real incomes. In a still longer period we may perhaps expect changes in the general business attitude, for instance, more vigorous competition.

The first source of empirical evidence may be seen in the *experience with Benelux:* as early as 1948, Belgium, Luxemburg and the Netherlands abolished most of their mutual trade impediments. Professor P. J. Verdoorn made a thorough analysis of this experience[1] and found two important features of this process of integration. First of all, the pattern of the changes in trade showed a much «finer» structure than was sometimes believed. Increased competition did not lead to uniform increases in all items within one industry in one

1. P. J. VERDOORN, «*The Intra-Block Trade of Benelux*», paper presented at the Lisbon meeting of the International Economic Association, Lisbon, 1957.

direction or the other, but to increases in a large number of items and decreases in a large number of other items within the same industry. Belgium «won» in many items within the textile industry, but the Netherlands in many other items; no industry was ruled out «en bloc». Secondly, Verdoorn found that the increase in trade, even after correction for the influence of other circumstances, considerably exceeded what could have been expected on the basis of our knowledge of demand elasticities and price reductions. In other words, the observed shifts can only be explained by elasticities which are greater than usual or by an additional willingness to trade, due, it seems, to the awareness of traders that these tariff reductions will not be reversed any more.

In another study, Verdoorn[2] tried to estimate the effects of the establishment of the European Economic Community on the mutual trade between the six member countries, using the price reductions to be expected and the demand elasticities known so far as his basis. In the light of what we have just stated this may be an underestimation. The result of the estimation shows an expected increase in trade between member countries of some 20 per cent.

The *increase in efficiency* to be expected on the somewhat longer term has been the subject of even cruder guesses. The order of magnitude has been estimated at a few per cent of national product. One should bear in mind that increased efficiency can only be expected in industries for which integration means an enlargement of their markets. This will not apply to industries with a local market, such as bakeries, or those with national markets and a uniform product. The crucial phenomenon will be the possibility of producing a smaller number of products as a consequence of specialization. This may be no more than 20 per cent of all production. If in such industries a cost decrease of say 25 per cent can be obtained – which is a considerable decrease – the increase in efficiency for the economy as a whole will be some 5 per cent.

Over and above an increase in efficiency, well-being may be increased by a *more intense exchange* of qualities between countries; but the order of magnitude of this effect will not exceed one per cent of national

2. P. J. Verdoorn, *Welke zijn de achtergronden en vooruitzichten van de economische integratie in Europa, etc.*, The Hague, 1952.

income. The total effect on well-being of the two factors mentioned will therefore remain modest.

Finally, the extent to which a change in attitude, such as a more intensive competitive attitude, may further raise production remains completely uncertain. Suggestions, such as those made by Professor Maurice Allais, to the effect that a doubling of production might be hoped for, are based on the assumption that most of the difference between American and European prosperity can be attributed to such a difference in attitude and that the establishment of the European Economic Community would bring about, in Europe, an American level of competitive activity. This seems very doubtful.

9 – MONETARY INTEGRATION

9.1 – After having discussed the use to be made of the instruments of economic policy that, as such, directly influence current transactions between nations, we will now deal with the *monetary instruments,* i.e. with the techniques of international payments and their integration. From the nature of the matter and its treatment in the analytical chapters it will be clear that current transactions may be directly influenced also by any regulations with regard to their payment; transactions that cannot be paid for have little chance of being repeated. The central question behind this theme is, of course, what organization of international payments deserves preference. From chapter 5, in particular, it will be clear that this organization has to depend on the fulfilment of certain equilibrium conditions, without which a payments system cannot work. We will come back to these conditions in a moment.

Assuming that they are fulfilled, it is clear that the simplest and, therefore, theoretically the best organization of international payments would be the introduction of a *world currency*. This is a very appealing idea, especially to the layman. With a world currency, no transformation of one type of money into another would be necessary and all the trouble connected with it – changes in exchange rates and their risks, inconvertibility – could be avoided, seemingly. It is often forgotten that such a world currency could work only if certain rather rigorous conditions of «good behaviour» were fulfilled [which some people think they could dispense with under a world currency]. If these conditions were fulfilled, a system of convertible national currencies could work just as smoothly. The main condition is that there should be spending equilibrium for each separate area, i.e. equality between income and expenditure, to the extent that such an area did not receive deliberate «help» from others or have reserves at its disposal. For the word «area» we could also read, in this connection, «group of families» or «group of enterprises» or, finally, «one family» or «one enterprise». A world currency, in other words, would not help any individual or any group to overcome a deficit in his or its finance, if nobody was inclined to help.

In a way, a world currency would, therefore, be a rigorous means of enforcing spending equilibrium on those who have no reserves. This is the very reason why most national governments would not like to hand over their sovereign rights to create money; they want to be free to make deficits if their policy implies such deficits. Only if there were complete political homogeneity between the national governments and the central financial authority could no difficulties arise. This implies that agreement could be obtained, at any time, on the extra help that certain governments should receive or on the amounts some governments would have to make available to others. Therefore, the necessary prerequisite would be that there already be political unity, and that the machinery to deal with such questions existed and worked sufficiently smoothly.

Apart from these conditions, it is doubtful whether, in a world *threatened by wars,* even a set of allied countries could permit itself the «luxury» of one common currency. Such a currency could be upset by any general attempt at the flight of capital from, say, threatened areas. No new investments would, perhaps, be made at all in such areas if the world currency system made it possible to use savings for investment in remote parts of the world without any permission. Some division into «watertight» compartments, as far as capital movements are concerned, would seem indispensable.

9.2 – If, then, the condition of spending equilibrium is fulfilled for current transactions and the permissible capital transactions taken together, a system of national currencies can yield, without much trouble, almost the same services as are expected for these transactions and, hence, there will be no hindrance of normal intercourse.

It cannot be denied, however, that the problem of *changes in exchange rates* nevertheless remains a problem with several aspects. On the one hand, the possibility of changing rates provides an opportunity to regulate the price level of separate countries in order to adapt their competitive position to changed conditions. On the other hand, it means the existence of certain risks for trade, especially if the changes can be large. It is not easy to construct a system without any drawbacks. The system of *flexible exchange rates* has the advantage of smooth and, hence, small changes but the disadvantages of, for example, speculative deviations, which are difficult to eliminate completely, and arbitrariness in short-term policy. During the later depression years of the thirties this system was advocated because of the impact of the extensive price movements, which – it was hoped – would be avoided by changes in exchange rates. Upon closer consideration and assuming a better anti-cyclic policy, experts have, since the war, generally turned towards a system of fixed rates which would only need incidental adjustments. This has been made the basis of the International Monetary Fund.

Present-day national monetary systems do not use only gold as a reserve but, in addition, so-called «key» currencies, such as dollar and sterling values. This system of key currencies, known also as the gold exchange system, has some disadvantages, which have been clearly set out by Professor Robert Triffin[1]. The supply of such currencies will depend on the balance of payments position of their home country. More dollars will be made available whenever there is a deficit in the balance of payments of the United States and less will be made available if this country shows a surplus on its foreign accounts. This means that there will be a tendency to use more of this key currency whenever its position threatens to become weak or less of it whenever its position tends to be strong. Such a structure is unstable. A considerable deterioration of a key currency may undermine confidence in it and then make other countries decide to switch to another reserve currency, which will suddenly further undermine its position. A more stable structure requires the use of some international paper for reserve purposes, for instance, IMF bonds or bills.

9.3 – Since, in our terminology, changes in exchange rates are conflicting instruments of economic policy, they should be under some control from an international agency, and their use should be restricted. Such is the theory of the Bretton Woods Agreement on which the International Monetary Fund is based. In practice, so far, not very much «control» has been possible. Of course, there is some hesitation

1. R. Triffin, *Gold and the Dollar Crisis – Future of Convertibility,* Yale University Press, New Haven, 1960.

on the part of governments to use the instrument of devaluation, since it will hardly be considered a glorious achievement of the country applying it; but, when applied, it is almost autonomously applied. Perhaps the only conceivable brake to be applied to changes which are too frequent and too big would be a set of sanctions in the field of credits.

A prerequisite of a minimum of changes in rates is, as has already been observed, equilibrium in the balances of payments. Apart from a complete regulation of all transactions – not very attractive to Western countries – this will, in the short run, only be possible if sufficient reserves are available. These may be partly centralized in an international «equalization fund» such as the International Monetary Fund.

In the long run, equilibrium can only be maintained if, as was set out in chapter 7, national economic policy is one of spending equilibrium at a high level of employment. This not only implies a certain financial policy directed towards spending equilibrium but, at the same time, a certain *price and wage policy* directed towards the maintenance of competitive power. Only with such a price and wage policy will it be possible to avoid changes in exchange rates. In many countries recent trends have been towards a great rigidity in wages and prices, as a consequence of increased organization of the labour market and of the markets of many industrial and agricultural products. Adaptability is further hampered by cost-of-living clauses in labour contracts and similar attempts to maintain the purchasing power of incomes under all circumstances. The question may be put as to whether this is, in the end, a desirable policy. Experience in the Netherlands gives some encouragement to those who believe that an improved understanding of the functioning of the economy, on the part of trade unions and employers' unions, may make it possible to reduce price and wage rigidity. The workers should also be confident that if adjustments are necessary they will be applied to all groups in an equitable way. Such confidence can only exist if there are certain standards of decency in economic negotiations, together with a well-balanced political system in which all groups of the population participate. Without such possibilities for the reduction of price and wage rigidity there will be no chance, apart from adjustments in capital movements, of avoiding adjustments in exchange rates.

9.4 – *Capital movements,* in fact, may have an important equilibrating function. *Short-term* capital movements were already implied, to some extent, when we spoke of the functions of reserves and of an international equalization fund. Private short-term capital movements will be possible in so far as trade credits can be somewhat adapted to the situation. The other types of private short-term capital movements, which played an important role in the quiet periods of the nineteenth century, are generally considered less helpful in a world where fresh disturbances may arise for political reasons. They may then take the form of «hot money» moving nervously from one financial centre to another and often doing more harm than good. In the present time of restricted freedom of capital movements they have been more or less eliminated and, therefore, are not able to exert any equilibrating force either.

There remain *long-term* capital movements, both private and public. Although these usually will have another primary objective, they nevertheless do, or can, also have a function in the maintenance of equilibrium in the balance of payments. It is only natural that countries with a surplus of savings should supply capital to countries with a deficit in capital formation. By a surplus of savings we mean a surplus in relation to the investments that should be made at home, judged from the international economic point of view in the widest sense. If for political or psychological reasons, say fear of war risks, such a capital transfer does not take place in the private sphere, there may be scope for public action. Some of the well-known disequilibria of the post-war period [both «dollar scarcity» and «dollar abundance»] have, in this way, been remedied to some extent.

In order that capital movements should be an equilibrating and not a disequilibrating factor, certain conditions have also to be fulfilled regarding the distribution of a country's assets and liabilities over the various «*degrees of liquidity*». The amounts due for amortization should correspond to the amounts available per period of time. Difficult situations have sometimes arisen because of lack of such correspondence. Germany in 1931 had short-term debts against illiquid assets. The «sterling balances» accumulated during World War II in a number of countries of the Commonwealth should, from the debtor's standpoint, have been long-term debts, since there was no possibility for Britain to pay them off in a short period. There was a tendency for the creditor countries, however, to spend part of the balance in a short time, especially in so far as they wanted to apply it for reconstruction purposes. This lack of correspondence had to be removed either by a change in the status of the balances or by compensatory provisions such as foreign loans, before sterling could be made convertible.

9.5 – The Second World War caused serious disturbances to spending equilibria. Important shifts in assets occurred as a consequence of the financing of the war; Great Britain sold considerable amounts of her foreign investments, partly to American citizens. She also incurred considerable debts to countries such as India, Australia and Egypt. The productive capacities of the war-stricken countries were seriously reduced, simultaneously with the creation of internal debts and money. Both in Europe and in Asia serious balance of payments deficits occurred. The United States gave very considerable assistance to European countries, especially through the European Recovery Program (or Marshall Plan); this enabled the Western European countries to rebuild their economies and to increase their exports. Until 1950 the payments of these countries had to be kept under strict control, in the beginning only by means of bilateral agreements. Gradually, the payments system could be made more multilateral, initially by a complicated system of clearing activities and later by re-introducing convertibility. The process was, on the payments side, organized by the European Payments Union [EPU] and, on the trade side, by the Organization for European Economic Cooperation [OEEC]. In 1958 the Treaty of Rome created the European Economic Community [EEG] of Benelux, France, Germany and Italy; seven other countries established the European Free Trade Area [EFTA]. European economies had regained strength, and some of their currencies, especially the Dutch and German currencies, became «stronger» than the dollar, as demonstrated by their revaluation in 1961.

While for about ten years after World War II the balance of payments of the United States had shown surpluses on current account, to the extent even that several economists considered this a permanent feature, the position of the dollar gradually began to deteriorate and around 1960 heavy deficits developed, which it appeared, were equally difficult to eliminate.

The position of most developing countries remained weak. India,

Pakistan and Egypt [later the United Arab Republic] could make use of their sterling balances in the beginning, but these were soon exhausted. Prices of primary commodities, which had risen during and immediately after the war, received another fillip from the Korea crisis but, from 1951 on, declined, to the detriment of the balances of payments of the developing countries. Since 1950 increasing amounts of public financial assistance have been given to them by the developed countries, amounting to $ 6 milliards [American: billions] in 1961, but it has remained necessary for most developing countries to apply payments controls.

9.6 – There is scope, therefore, for further integration of the payments systems of the non-communist world, whose international structure may be improved by three main groups of measures. To begin with, the developed countries may facilitate the payments position of the less developed ones by a *further increase in long-term investments and aid.* This subject will be discussed in more detail in Chapter 10. Then, the International Monetary Fund may continue to increase the *availability of liquidities* and may develop more systematic methods to adapt liquidity creation to the need for liquidity. So far, the measures taken have been rather of an incidental nature. To be sure, none of the systems so far used or proposed has the effect of mechanically producing the necessary volume of money circulation. As long as gold and key currencies are the basis for money circulation and some significance is attached to legal or conventional ratios between reserves and circulation, the latter will depend on a number of arbitrary factors, such as the production of gold, the supply of gold by the Soviet Union or the balance of payments deficit of the United States or Britain. Some element of planning and a declaration of intent by the International Monetary Fund might be a better basis, irrespective of the precise techniques used to create liquidities. Finally, a contribution must also be made by the developing countries, many of which are in need of a better financial structure. To a considerable extent, this boils down to the necessity to *raise more taxes* and to raise the *tax morals,* especially of high-income groups.

10.1 – So far, international economic policy has been discussed on the basis of a *given distribution of resources,* i.e. land and capital, over nations. As has already been stated in chapter 1, this distribution is, however, far from satisfactory; it is extremely uneven if calculated per head of population. This inequality is due partly to artificial impediments to the movement of the factors of production, especially to the movement of population. In addition, it is probably due to differences in mental attitudes and abilities between nations. However that may be, this extreme inequality is becoming an important source of future tensions. Traffic between nations has increased, as have communications generally; people are more and more becoming conscious of the great differences and less and less willing to take them for granted. They are helped in this attitude by communist propaganda. A complication is the increasing rather than decreasing divergence of standards of living. Whereas some young underdeveloped countries are struggling with the problems created by their newly obtained independence and, thereby, are stagnating in economic development, the leading developed countries are increasing production even more rapidly than before. This divergence in standards of living threatens political stability in the world at large and constitutes a major challenge to our economic regime.

10.2 – It has been believed that there are *automatic forces* at work towards an equalization of welfare. One of the well-known arguments is that of «factor price equalization». The argument states that the specialization of wealthy countries in the sphere of the capital-intensive industries and of poorer countries in the sphere of the labour-intensive industries will make it possible for the same wage rate and the same interest rate to be paid in both types of countries. This specialization, it is maintained, only requires free trade in final products, which may take the place of movements of population or capital. As has been shown by further research, this argument has only limited validity. It is not of general validity and depends on the figures involved. If the differences in capital intensity between industries are smaller than the differences between countries, the equalization of wages and interest is not possible. What is also relevant in this context is that some of the more capital-intensive industries produce products that cannot be transported at all and have to be produced inside each country [e.g. electrivity, transport services, «housing services»].

An even greater difficulty arises if the capital intensities of the various conceivable industries [i.e. the ratio of the quantity of capital available to the quantity of labour] are each of them higher than the capital intensity of the country. In this case, the lack of capital even makes it impossible to employ all the labour. In such a situation we may speak of an «*absolute scarcity of capital*».

It may be safely stated that, as long as factors are not permitted to move much more intensely than today, there is not much hope for an equalization of wages and interest rates or even for full employment of labour. The only solution to the problem of diverging standards of living lies in a greater movement of factors. Essentially, what is needed is the integration of the process of development. The growth of a country should not be considered a problem only of concern to that one country, which it has to solve entirely with its own investments. It is part of a world problem of equilibrated growth. It should be recognized that the problem is partly one of population policy. If populations had increased less rapidly in the poorer countries, their welfare would certainly have been higher. One indispensable element of the solution consists of the recognition of this fact and the willingness to apply what the Indian government calls «family planning».

10.3 – In some quarters it has been believed that the standards of living of the poorer countries could be raised *by decree*, so to speak. It was believed that the prescription of higher wages and the equalization of the labour conditions, generally, would be a step towards eliminating «social dumping». This is a misunderstanding of the economic forces at work. The main effect of such measures would be to reduce the number of workers that can be employed at all in such

91

countries. Higher standards of living for the population as a whole can only be obtained from *increases in production*. A considerable rise in production can only be obtained by considerable increases in capital invested and in training, and by the spread of technical knowledge. Consumption aid for an enormous population such as that of Asia would have to be so large, if the remedy had to come from such aid, that it would be out of the question. Whatever contributions obtained would have to be used for investment as far as possible and, even then, very considerable amounts would be needed [cf. section 10.4]. The investments most needed are of the «basic» type, i.e. for the improvement of the productive basis of the country: land improvement, irrigation, supply of energy, improvement of the transport system and of education and housing. Many of these investments are hardly remunerative in the private sense of the word. However, they appear to be the decisive element which makes less industrialized countries attractive for further investment. Once they exist, all production is easier.

The need for a considerable effort to increase production has now been understood by most low-income countries. Their deliberate development has been made the central theme of their economy and social policies. An increasing number of these countries have established a development plan, usually extending over at least five years and often being followed by more than one such plan. As a rule, such plans call for increased investment and an increase in education expenditure and education effort.

It is, however, virtually impossible to increase the capital formation of the underdeveloped countries until it is sufficient to meet even the demands of a modest development program. The reason is to be found in the low per capita income in these countries, out of which little can be saved. This is a self-evident phenomenon also observable inside every developed country. The poor do not save. Only the high-income groups can and do save; but their numbers are very small in these countries. Of course, no attempt to increase savings should be neglected; but it would not be realistic to expect much from this source.

10.4 – It is now generally recognized that the accelerated development of the low-income countries constitutes *World Economic Problem*

Number One. This has been expressed in, among other policy declarations, the solemn inauguration by the United Nations General Assembly of the « *Development Decade* ». The document summarizing the aims and means of such an international policy formulates as its most important aim the increase in national incomes of the developing countries by 50 per cent. Among the means, a capital transfer of 1 per cent of the national incomes of the developed countries, representing some $ 8 milliards for 1960 and some $ 12 milliards for 1970, is mentioned.

It must be feared that both the formulation of the aim and the level of this capital transfer are insufficient to solve the real problem at stake, that is, the divergence in real incomes per head between the developed and the developing countries. In addition, it remains doubtful whether the member countries will live up to the standard required from them. In order to attain convergence in incomes per head the capital flow will have to be more than 1 per cent, maybe 1.5 or 2 per cent of the incomes of the developed countries. Only a moderate portion of this amount can be supplied by private investors. At present, some $ 3 milliards are invested by the private sector. The remainder must be taken care of by public institutions. This public contribution should be distributed in an equitable way over the developed countries, taking into account their level of well-being. A key for such a distribution may be found in any of the income tax schedules now in use in the developed countries.

Some of the financial transfers to the developing countries may take the form of loans. There remains scope for a considerable portion of contributions in other forms. More particularly, there is a need for an international *ordinary budget* which disburses investment expenditure as a current policy at the international level. Some arguments for this particular type of financing will be offered in section 11.7.

10.5 – As already briefly mentioned, development policies are increasingly being based on a *national development plan*. It is a prerequisite for an efficient use of capital and manpower that no idle capacity of either be created. This requires careful calculation of the rates of growth of different sectors, of the increases in school capacities, teachers and pupils, and careful appraisal of investment projects from a national point of view. In many countries such plans now exist or are in preparation. For their proper construction they need not only many figures of a national character, but also a considerable amount of data on the prospective development of other countries and of world markets. For this purpose and also for the purpose of creating the basis of an international economic policy, an *international development plan* is needed. At present, the preparatory activities for such a plan are in progress. The United Nations Secretariat is preparing projections of a number of important variables representing the main features of the world economy and is studying methods to create an international network of information and communication on such matters. A world development plan may be the basis for annual discussions on international and national economic policies in Ecosoc and in the United Nations Assembly. Such a plan may also be of great help for the most efficient development of the heavy industries in developing continents. The optimum size of enterprises in these industries usually exceeds the absorptive capacity of national markets. In order to arrive at the most efficient structure, on the one hand, and at an equitable distribution of income among developing countries, on the other hand, agreements about the establishment of such enterprises between a number of neighbouring countries may be concluded. These can best be negotiated by combined deals, implying enterprises in different industries, so as to make it possible for each country to receive some industrial activity of this type. For such agreements an international plan will be useful.

As a matter of course, the products of such enterprises should be freely traded between the countries concluding the agreement. We may call such an agreement a *«partial customs union cum investment plan»*. It is desirable that the Contracting Parties to GATT should accept this type of customs union, provided it is, in fact, combined with an investment plan distributing the enterprises over the countries who are parties to the agreement.

10.6 – An important subject to be dealt with in an international development plan is the future division of labour between developed and less developed countries. Basically, it is always possible to let all industries in all countries operate at full capacity. The condition to be fulfilled is that the distribution of new investment over the various industries should correspond to the distribution over the same industries of the additional demand to be expected from additional incomes. In order to maximize world income we must, moreover, let every country have the industries in which it has the highest comparative advantages. It seems probable that the developed countries will have to leave to the developing ones the labour-intensive industries of relatively small optimum size, whereas the former will hold on to the industries requiring a relatively large amount of research and highly developed skills and having a large optimum size.

11.1 – In the preceding chapters a system of international economic policy directed towards integration was described. The degree of centralization needed for the execution of the corresponding tasks was also discussed. We will now discuss what *agencies* will have to be charged with these tasks, to what extent the existing national agencies will be able to perform them and to what extent these will have to be or have already been switched over to existing international agencies. To what extent, finally, will there be a need for new international agencies? This problem of the *organization of international economic policy* is ultimately connected with the problem of political integration, which may be said also to represent a problem of «optimum centralization». A politically integrated area is the ideal area for the application of an integrated economic policy, and vice versa; the two aspects can hardly be divorced. In this respect it is useful to distinguish between the integration of the economies and the integration of economic policy itself. An integrated economic policy presupposes the existence of a «*common policy*» or a «harmonized policy». Therefore, part of the integration process consists of a discussion between parties as to which policy they are all able to follow. The common policy has to be, of necessity, a compromise; the best compromise will be one which can be based on certain scientific principles of consistency. Even then, of course, the common policy may be less interventionist or more interventionist, according to the prevailing tastes in this respect and according to the circumstances. In times of serious disequilibria a more interventionist policy might be preferred to the one prevailing in times of equilibrium.

Unfortunately, there are many discrepancies between the ideal degree of co-operation which has been assumed in our discussion and the attitudes of the parties involved. The peoples – or only the governments, or both – may not yet be prepared to co-operate to the extent which might be desirable for purely economic reasons. They also may not be prepared to co-operate to the extent to which their own long-term interests would seem to require political integration. In all such circumstances, other solutions than the optimum ones will have to be accepted, if only temporarily or as a first step. Moreover, we should not exclude the possibility that experience about co-operation would in the end teach something to all concerned, including the advocates of integration. Instead of a central organ for a certain function, the choice may be limited to a co-ordination of the policies of decentralized organs or to consultations only in particular circumstances. Our discussion in this chapter will be based on the assumption that the desire for co-operation exists. It may, accordingly, sometimes be biassed in order to contribute to the further development of that desire.

Tasks which are only of *local or national* interest should, of course, be left to local or national organs; this is a generally accepted democratic principle. As was set out in section 6.4, it is primarily where one goverment may adversely of favourably affect the interests of other nations that a *central agency* will be needed. It is conceivable that certain agencies should be *regional,* in the sense of embracing only a group of neighbouring countries instead of all countries concerned. In so far as an agency has a task with regard to a «conflicting» instrument of economic policy [the first case just mentioned], its job may primarily be a *supervising* one. In this case, as we maintained previously, the abolition of the use of the instrument which requires supervision may be the best form of centralization. In the second case, i.e. that of a supporting instrument, a more *active operation* may be needed. Since many instruments may be alternately conflicting and supporting, both types of tasks have often to be envisaged. Agencies should be created, as is implied in the foregoing remarks, according to the instruments of economic policy rather than according to the aims of that policy. Each instrument will have to be handled with a view to its contribution to all the targets of policy; and each target will have to be attained with the help of several instruments. If there were an agency for each target, an enormous confusion would be created as to who would have to decide on the use of a certain instrument. Therefore, it is correct that there should be agencies supervising tariffs or exchange rates, since these are instruments. It would not be correct to have an agency dealing with employment policy, which is a target; instead there should be agencies which decide upon public expenditure, taxes, etc., which may be the instruments of economic policy. The agency dealing with expenditure, however, would have to base its decisions not only on the employment target, but on other targets as well. Even then, every target could be taken care of provided the number of targets does not exceed the number of instruments.

Finally, instruments and agencies may be subdivided into *general* and *partial* ones: the general ones having to do with economies as a whole and the partial ones with certain sectors only, e.g. coal and steel production. It will be clear that the well-being of the sectors may depend to a very high degree on the handling of general instruments. Partial agencies may have a vital interest, therefore, in the creation of certain general agencies which handle instruments of importance to them.

From our survey of economic policy in chapters 8–10 it has become clear that general agencies will be needed particularly for:

[1] the supervision and reduction of *trade restrictions*,

[2] the regulation of *raw material markets*,

[3] the supervision of the *convertibility of currencies*,

[4] the supervision of *spending equilibrium* and *employment* policy,

[5] the supply of capital for *development*,

[6] the transfer of *knowledge* and *education* assistance, and

[7] the regulation of *migration*.

In principle, all these tasks should be performed on a *world basis,* although some may also be subject to co-operation on a *regional* basis, supervision being given at the world level. In view of the unhappy controversy between the communist and the non-communist countries, co-operation between only a restricted number of countries may prove possible. Regional integration may be useful, if certain instruments of economic policy are used only by a regional group of countries; this may be so either because other countries prefer not to use them or are not able to use them. A condition which, of course, must be fulfilled is that the nature of the problem to be solved should also be regional and not world-wide. Regional regulation of a market with world-wide competition would, for example, not be possible.

In principle, agencies have been created by the United Nations for each of the main tasks indicated; but various difficulties have been encountered.

11.2 – *The supervision and reduction of trade restrictions* should have been the task of the *International Trade Organization* [ITO]. However, it has not come into existence, despite extensive preparatory work, mainly because of the reluctance of the United States to accept the amended charter. Although the tasks with regard to trade restrictions have been taken over by the *General Agreement on Trade and Tariffs* [GATT], it cannot be said that the process of reduction of restrictions has been very successful. This applies both to quantitative restrictions and tariffs. Two main factors are responsible for these difficulties: [i] the unwillingness of many countries to move faster in the direction of free trade and [ii] the extremely complicated technique adopted to negotiate reductions in tariffs. The common root of both causes is the divergence of interests connected with the existence of tariffs. Therefore, there is a tendency to maintain certain tariffs of vital importance to some industries and a reluctance, on the part of governments, to accept simple schemes for the general reduction of tariffs. Lack of determination and of a somewhat broader outlook in connection with these problems remains another handicap to integration.

Considerable progress has been made within Europe, first by the activities of the Organization for European Economic Co-operation [OEEC] [now known as the Organization for Economic Co-operation and Development or OECD] and later by the European Economic Community [EEC], comprising only part of the Western European countries. Between the Benelux countries, France, Germany and Italy the Treaty of Rome has been concluded for the establishment of a customs union and a number of common institutions in other fields. Prospects for a reduction of trade impediments over a wider area have been opened up by the possibility of membership or association for other countries. Such prospects have also been opened up by a recent initiative of the American Government which calls for the authorization to negotiate «linear» reductions in tariffs, that is, reductions applied to a large group of commodities at once.

The Treaty of Rome aims at an elimination of tariffs and quantitative restrictions between its member countries but maintains the average level of the existing tariffs vis-à-vis the outside world. By so doing and because of the possibility of association, it creates, however, a discrimination against non-associated countries, especially those competing with the associated territories. The non-associated countries of

99

Africa and Latin America are threatened by this development. Discussions and negotiations to mitigate its consequences have been started. The best solution consists of a *lowering of the external tariff of the EEC*.

A special difficulty exists in the field of *textiles*. The sharp competition experienced by the European textile industry from newly developing countries has led to severe quantitative restrictions on the imports of cotton textiles of certain denominations originating from Japan, India, Pakistan and Hong Kong. Considerable pressure has been exerted on the European countries applying these quantitative restrictions. Several governments are reluctant to yield to this pressure. The Cotton Textiles Agreement concluded in 1962 only slightly relaxes the restrictions. This is not yet a very satisfactory situation from an international point of view. It is highly desirable that developing countries increase their exports of the goods in which they have a cost advantage.

11.3 – *The regulation of raw material markets* is entrusted, at the world level, to the Food and Agriculture Organization [FAO] for agricultural products and the Committee for International Commodity Trade of the United Nations for mining products. At the level of the EEC the latter organization is developing its common agricultural policy and the European Coal and Steel Community supervises the coal and steel and some related markets. For a limited number of commodities, commodity agreements are in operation; these regulate, to some extent, the markets for wheat, sugar, tin, coffee and tea. The systems of regulation chosen are all different. Thus, for wheat, limits are imposed on exports and imports as well as on prices. In a period of scarcity, certain minimum quantities must be made available by exporters and there is a ceiling to the price; in periods of abundance, certain minimum amounts must be imported by the importing countries and there is a floor to the price. In the case of tin, a buffer stock is operated in an attempt to keep the price as stable as possible.

For many other commodities attempts to secure an agreement have not been successful so far. Governments have not been willing to commit themselves, mainly as a consequence of pressure groups. In periods of rising prices, exporting countries are not interested, while in periods of falling prices, importing countries are not interested. The history of these attempts has been a first-class demonstration of short-sightedness, but some improvement in the negotiating climate took place around 1962.

However, one may ask whether simpler solutions to the main problem are not available. One currently considered scheme was proposed to the Secretary General of the United Nations by a group of experts; this plan provides a possibility for governments to *insure* themselves against *declines in export receipts* for their countries taken as a whole. In this scheme, all member countries pay an annual contribution of a few tenths of one per cent of their national income; in return, they obtain the right to receive compensation from the central fund whenever their export receipts are less than 97.5 per cent of the average of the last three years. This compensation may be either the full amount by which exports fall short of this standard or it may be a fixed portion of it; the contributions mentioned earlier must of course be geared to the choice made here.

11.4 – *The supervision of the convertibility of currencies* and a number of related tasks are entrusted to the International Monetary Fund. Among the related tasks are important information, research and consulting tasks as well as the approval of changes in the par value of the currency of a member country when it exceeds a certain limit. The Fund's main function is to make available short-term credits to member countries in order to overcome temporary shortages in foreign currencies. There are certain limits to what any single country can obtain, but these limits evidently depend, among other things, on the means available to the Fund. In the course of the Fund's existence these means have been increased substantially, but in some quarters the feeling is that they are still too small. Many Central Bank officials are of the opposite opinion.

The Fund cannot help any country to overcome permanent payments difficulties by long-term credits. In the case of a «fundamental disequilibrium» in a country's balance of payments it can approve a devaluation of that country's currency, in the case of a deficit, or a revaluation, in the case of a surplus.

We have already discussed [section 9.2] the question of whether the present *structure* of the international payments system satisfies the conditions ideally imposed upon such a system and the answer given by Professor Triffin. It seems very doubtful whether the system of key currencies should be chosen as the final system. An attempt at establishing the best international system irrespective of existing vested interests may well require the creation of a really supra-national central bank with its own «paper», that is, bonds or bills which may serve as reserve material for national central banks.

There remains another fundamental question, discussed in section 9.6, concerning the *most desirable volume of liquidities available*. As explained, this cannot be created automatically by the adherence to any rules of fixed reserve ratios since the production of gold depends on factors not relevant to this problem. The most desirable volume of liquidities can only be the outcome of a planned approach, taking the most desirable development of production, prices and payment habits as its elements.

11.5 – *The supervision of spending equilibrium and employment policies* is less clearly the task of an existing international agency. These policies are to a large extent left to the national governments and, clearly, the largest countries [in terms of national income and international trade] will exert the most important influence on the international economic situation. There is some co-ordination, but it is not a very strong form. The strongest forms of co-ordination so far applied are those of the periodic «examinations» within the OEEC and the OECD and of the Monetary Committee of the EEC. Some consultation exists between Central Bank presidents. At the world level, the annual discussion in the Ecosoc plays a similar role, but represents a very weak form of co-ordination. If, at this level, the method of the OEEC and the OECD were applied, real progress could be made. This method consists of a thorough analysis of each country's policies by representatives of two other countries and an open discussion finishing up with recommendations to the government examined. In the past these recommendations have had some influence.

Even so, stronger forms of co-ordination are desirable. The aims at stake are among the most important aims of economic policy. Wrong policies will not only affect the country concerned but many other countries, too; consequently, they cannot be left to national governments alone. We will discuss one possible international instrument in section 11.7.

11.6 – The *task of supplying capital to developing countries* is carried out by various agencies with differing degrees of centralization. Some developed countries have important bilateral programs, such as the United States Point Four and consecutive programs, now handled by the AID [Agency of International Development]. There are also programs carried out by groups of countries. Thus, the Colombo Plan is a program initiated by countries of the British Commonwealth but at present also having members not belonging to that group, for instance Indonesia; the Colombo Plan operates in South-East Asia. The EEC has its Development Bank, supplying capital to the less developed parts of European countries, and its Development Fund, supplying capital to the associated countries outside Europe. The Alliance for Progress is an inter-American institution directed at the development of Latin American countries.

Various institutions operate at the highest international level. The U.N. Special Fund is of a very modest size and finances pre-investment activities such as exploration and education schemes. By far the most important agency is the International Bank for Reconstruction and Development, which supplies loans at market conditions to governments for development purposes. Moreover, the Bank administers two other agencies, namely, the International Finance Corporation and the International Development Association. The former helps to finance private corporations by investing in them; these investments it later sells, thus creating a revolving fund. The latter supplies loans to governments at below market conditions and hence has to be financed by public funds. The activities of these three connected agencies have increased considerably since 1950. Even so, there remains scope for further increases.

11.7 – Of the set of agencies in the monetary and financial field, one institution is lacking which, at the national level, is usually the most important of all, namely, a *Treasury* or Ministry of Finance. Essentially, the activities of a Treasury are to collect current revenues and to spend them on current account; these activities are carried out both for their own sake and in order to help maintain full employment and monetary equilibrium, where necessary, in co-operation with other instruments of economic policy. There seems to be scope for the creation of such an agency at the international level. This could be a significant contribution to the strength of international order; in fact, only financial power will make an agency powerful. The two initial tasks which an International Treasury could perform are [i] the operation of the insurance scheme discussed in section 11.3 and [ii] the disbursement, out of taxes collected from U.N. member governments, of some investment expenditure of international importance; this expenditure can be justified because it covers projects comprising several nations and because it helps to develop a nation in the interests of the world as a whole. These operations could be so distributed over time as to contribute to the elimination of cycles and so distributed over the world's areas as to contribute to a more equitable distribution of world income.

11.8 – The *transmission of knowledge and education assistance* are tasks performed by various institutions belonging to the United Nations family. Technological knowledge of a specialized nature is often transmitted by the corresponding specialized agency. Agricultural know-how is transmitted in many ways by the FAO, medical knowledge by the World Health Organization [WHO], monetary and financial knowledge by IMF, knowledge on social and labour matters by the International Labour Office [ILO], and so on. Technical assistance on economic policy, on economic development and planning and on industrialization, is transmitted by the IBRD and the U.N. Secretariat, whereas the various agencies mentioned often co-operate on the Technical Assistance Board.

Matters of education as such are, of course, the concern of the United Nations Educational, Scientific and Cultural Organization [UNESCO].

In recent years the importance of the transmission of knowledge and of education in all its ramifications has been increasingly understood. This has induced an organization such as the OECD to increase its activities in this field, even extending them to countries outside its own membership.

An international *regulation of migration* seems to be even more difficult to put into effect than the activities already mentioned. With respect to it international co-operation has completely broken down several times. Perhaps the biggest single cause of this lack of success is the rapid increase in population in the underdeveloped countries. Thus, some form of «family planning» will be indispensable, in the interests of all concerned. Difficult problems will have to be solved, but a dogmatic attitude will not contribute to any solution. A broad view and an open mind will be necessary for all the spiritual leaders concerned. Once the problem of population control has been recognized, the regulation of migration will become an easier task.

11.9 – If we try to *summarize* our findings and to draw some broad conclusions about the agencies of international economic integration, we can safely say that an important start has been made. The existing international agencies are the nuclei of co-operation around which the agencies needed for the future must «crystallize». However, the former are too small and have grown somewhat haphazardly, with only a little of the co-ordination which our analysis would indicate as being necessary. Even so, they already represent an impressive achievement, the purely technical difficulties of which are only too easily underestimated by the general public. If we have criticized their results, this does not mean that their limited success is their own fault. The overwhelming part of the fault lies with others. In many cases it is not the international «machinery» which is lacking, but rather the preparedness of governments to use it in the appropriate way. In most international negotiations it is usually the short-term or direct national interests which are taken as a criterion rather than the long-term and indirect interests – or international interests. It will be difficult for representatives of national governments to diverge very much from these narrower interests because, institutionally, they are forced to stick to them. The reason for so little progress can often be attributed to the very existence of national governments. To some extent, therefore, public opinion and its political expression in the parties will have to take the initiative and will have to urge the establishment of international parliamentary and governmental agencies. It will often be necessary for national governments and administrations [since they are the best equipped] to press for international co-operation agencies, because of the technical complexity of such activities. But they can only do so if they have the strong support of public opinion. Thus, two courses of action seem to be the most promising, namely, the type of broad-minded individual initiative from government quarters which led to the Marshall Plan, the Colombo Plan or the Schuman Plan, on the one hand, and a drive by political parties and ad hoc organizations to educate public opinion, on the other hand. Both should base themselves, at least partly, on the type of scientific analysis of the problems as has been attempted in this volume; i.e. an analysis which, it is hoped, will help one to judge which instruments of economic policy are most in need of centralization.

Our analysis in this respect has confirmed many viewpoints which, at present, govern the attempts at integration made both at the European level and, less clearly, at the world level. It has confirmed the desirability of a reduction in quantitative restrictions and in import duties, a positive integration of production, a certain unification of indirect taxes,convertibility of currencies, and an international policy of development. It has also confirmed that decentralization seems desirable for functions of a more local or national character. In addition to all this, the further conclusion has been reached that an essential element of integration will also have to be a higher degree of centralization in financial policy. This latter conclusion seems to be in accordance with what a long debate on internal economic policy has also taught, namely, that with more centralization in financial policy many other instruments of economic policy can be left decentralized.

READING LIST

READING LIST

The purpose of this list is a very restricted one, namely to indicate a few titles to those readers who want to have an «introduction» to modern economic literature in the fields touched upon in this text. Each of the publications mentioned contains further references to the literature. The titles are followed by a brief description for the reader's information.

American Economic Association [H. S. ELLIS and L. A. METZLER, ed.], *Readings in the Theory of International Trade,* London, 1950 [1953]. [Collection of some of the best scientific papers published during the last 20 years on the most important problems in the field of theory].

R. F. HARROD, *International Economics,* Cambridge, 1933 [1947]. [Brief text on the theory of international trade for students of economics].

L. H. JANSSEN, S. J., *Free Trade, Protection and Customs Union,* Leiden, 1961. [Clear and precise treatment of customs union, with numerical examples of mathematical formulae].

J. E. MEADE, *The Balance of Payments,* London, 1951. [Elaborate text, in simple language, on the international aspects of economic policy].

J. E. MEADE, *The Theory of Customs Unions,* Amsterdam, 1955. [Brief discussion, without mathematics, of fundamental questions of integration].

G. MYRDAL, *An International Economy,* New York, 1956. [Economic, political and sociological discussion of present problems of international co-operation and integration].

TRENDS in International Trade, *A Report by a Panel of Experts,* GATT, Geneva 1958.

UNITED NATIONS: *World Economic Survey* 1962, *I: The Developing Countries in World Trade.* [An excellent survey of the trade of developing countries and the impediments experienced].

In addition the following reports by experts invited by the U.N. Secretary General may be recommended:

1. *National and international measures for full employment;* report by a group of experts appointed by the Secretary General, Lake Success [United Nations, Dep. of Econ. Affairs], 1949.
2. *Measures for international economic stability;* report by a group of experts, New York [United Nations, Dep. of Econ. Affairs], 1951.
3. *Measures for the economic development of underdeveloped countries;* report by a group of experts appointed by the Secretary General of the United Nations, New York [United Nations, Dep. of Econ. Affairs], 1951.
4. *Commodity trade and economic development;* submitted by a Committee appointed by the Secretary-General, New York [United Nations, Dep. of Econ. Affairs], 1953.
5. *International compensation for fluctuations in commodity trade,* New York [United Nations, Dep. of Econ. and Social Affairs]. 1961.

APPENDICES I AND II

APPENDIX I – INTERNATIONAL TRADE
UNDER CONSTANT RETURNS IN A VERY SIMPLE
MODEL

In appendices 1 and 2 some basic theorems of the theory of international trade will be discussed for those who want to go into the
rigorous theoretical foundations of our subject matter. The treatment,
although exact, is still very simple and only represents an introduction
to modern theory in two of its aspects. The form of mathematics used
is mainly simple algebra and arithmetic in appendix 1 and graphical
analysis in appendix 2. The theory of international trade is composed
of a vast body of theorems bearing on situations and problems which
have many aspects. The discipline has grown rapidly in recent de-
cades and the need for co-ordination becomes stronger and stronger.
To the author it seems that four aspects in particular deserve attention
since they profoundly influence the structure of the problems. These
four aspects are:

[a] the «monetary» aspect [M]: is full employment [F] assumed
or is unemployment [U] accepted as a possibility?

[b] the «technical» aspect [T]: is production technology assumed to
be rigid [R] or are the production factors assumed to be sub-
stitutable [S]?

[c] the nature of «compartments» [C], i.e. the units of production
considered: are they industries connected with groups of products
[P] or representing only certain activities [A]? An example of the
latter approach, rather common in the theory of international
trade, is the procedure which only considers the imports of
finished products and combines imports of raw materials with
the exports of the corresponding products; in this case «pro-
cessing», an activity rather than a product, is made the sole basis of
study.

[d] the number of «compartments» [N]: is there only one [1] per
country, or more than one [j]?

Summarizing the aspects in the form the letter symbols indicated we
obtain

Aspects	M	T	C	N
Possible assumptions	F, U	R, S	P, A	i, j

A large number of combinations is possible and has in fact been dealt with by various theorists[1]. In our two appendices we will deal with two models which might both be characterized by the symbols:

$$F \quad R \quad A \quad 2$$

This means that, in both cases, full employment will be assumed throughout. A rigid relation between input and output will be assumed to exist; the nature of the compartments is that of activities [i.e. the imports of raw materials are disregarded as parts of imports] and there are two industries per country. The only difference is that in appendix 1 production processes are considered in which the relation between «output» and factor input is constant and the same for successive units of product [«constant returns»]. In appendix 2 this relationship is variable, admitting of «decreasing» and «increasing» returns. In appendix 1 a number of features are to be found which are characteristic both of classical theory and modern linear programming, but in the simplest conceivable form. It may be an easy introduction to both and, in particular, also to Professor FRANK D. GRAHAM's «Theory of International Values» [1948]. In appendix 2 some use is made of indifference curves and production theory. The latter represents a generalization in some respects and a limitation in others because the influence of bounds and inequalities [which are very important in appendix 1] is almost disregarded, as was usual in neo-classical analysis.

1. Of some recent models the following characteristic ones may be given in our symbols: P. A. SAMUELSON, «International Trade and the Equalisation of Factor Prices», *The Economic Journal*, 58 (1948), p. 163 and subsequent discussion by J. TINBERGEN and J. E. MEADE in *Metroeconomica*: model F S A (j).
M. FLEMING, «On Making the Best of Balance of Payments Restrictions on Imports», *The Economic Journal*, 61 (1951), p. 48 and subsequent discussion by J. TINBERGEN, «Four Alternative Policies to Restore Balance of Payments Equilibrium», *Econometrica*, 20 (1952), p. 372 and J. TINBERGEN and H. M. A. VAN DER WERFF, *Econometrica*, 21 (1953), p. 332: model F R A 1 (j).
F. MACHLUP, *International Trade and the National Income Multiplier*, Philadelphia, 1943, J. J. POLAK, *An International Economic System*, London, 1954, and L. A. METZLER, «A Multiplier-Region Theory of Income and Trade», *Econometrica*, 18 (1950), p. 329: model U R P 1.

From the foregoing remarks it will be clear how elementary the appendices are in comparison with the whole body of the theory of international trade. However, they do throw some light on the «main thesis» of free trade theory, and may stimulate the reader to further study.

The model to be discussed first will use arithmetic and simple algebra. It is given for the case of *one factor* of production [labour], two countries 1 and 2 [upper indices] and *two products* 1 and 2 [lower indices] produced in two different industries, also indicated by these lower indices. It is assumed that the number of hours of labour a_j^i needed to produce in country i one unit of product j remains *unchanged* whatever the number of units produced. The four figures will be taken as equal to

$$\begin{bmatrix} a_1^1 & a_2^1 \\ a_1^2 & a_2^2 \end{bmatrix} = \begin{bmatrix} 1 & 1.1 \\ 2.4 & 2 \end{bmatrix}$$

in our numerical examples.

Two types of situation will be considered. The first is an «*open*» situation in which the two countries are in contact with a world market which is large in comparison with their production and on which the two products have a price $= 1$. This model may be useful for the study of «small countries». A «*closed*» situation will also be considered, where only these two countries exist; here, one price, p_1, will be chosen equal to 1, since only relative prices matter in our problem.

The total number of workers in both countries, to be indicated by W^1 and W^2, is given [in our examples $W^1 = 10$, $W^2 = 20$] and it is assumed that they all are always employed. The number of workers in each «compartment» [i.e. an industry in a country] will be indicated by w_j^i. Sometimes it will be assumed that there is only a *limited* «*capacity to produce*» c_j^i in each compartment, i.e. that $w_j^i \leq c_j^i$ is a condition imposed on the number of workers. The reason may be a limitation imposed by some capital goods [with an infinite life and completely written off]. It is assumed that there is *free competition* between employers, leading to a wage rate l^i in each country which equals the marginal product of labour. The employers may not have any income at all as a consequence of this competition.

In the «open» problems, demand for the two products is evidently infinitely elastic; any quantity, that cannot be sold at home, can be sold «on the world market».

With the «closed» problems this is different; it will be assumed that demand satisfies two conditions:

[i] total income is spent; no more, no less

[ii] the ratio of the quantities demanded of both products is a function [equal in both countries] of the ratio of their prices.

Indicating by:

p_1^i and p_2^i the prices in country i of products 1 and 2,

y_1^i and y_2^i the quantities produced,

x_1^i and x_2^i the quantities demanded,

we will have the following relations:

[a] Income equals expenditure:

$$y_1^1 p_1 + y_2^1 p_2 = x_1^1 p_1 + x_2^1 p_2 \qquad [1]$$

$$y_1^2 p_1 + y_2^2 p_2 = x_1^2 p_1 + x_2^2 p_2 \qquad [2]$$

[b] Supply equals demand:

$$y_1^1 + y_1^2 = x_1^1 + x_1^2 \qquad [3]$$

$$y_2^1 + y_2^2 = x_2^1 + x_2^2 \qquad [4]$$

It is well known that, of these four equations, one is a consequence of the others; only three are independent.

[c] Relative demand is a function of relative prices:

$$\frac{x_1^1}{x_2^1} = \frac{x_1^2}{x_2^2} = c \frac{p_2}{p_1} + c_0 \qquad [5], [6]$$

where c and c_0 are constants.

[d] Supply follows from number of workers:

$$w_1^1 = a_1^1 y_1^1 \qquad w_2^1 = a_2^1 y_2^1 \qquad [7], [8]$$

$$w_1^2 = a_1^2 y_1^2 \qquad w_2^2 = a_2^2 y_2^2 \qquad [9], [10]$$

[e] All workers are employed:

$$w_1^1 + w_2^1 = W^1 \qquad w_1^2 + w_2^2 = W^2 \qquad [11], [12]$$

Here it has been assumed that prices p_1^1 and p_1^2 of product 1 are equal in both countries, and p_2^1 and p_2^2 as well. Without import duties this is correct, since we ignore transportation costs.

If import duties are introduced, prices need no longer be equal in the two countries. We will use the symbols p_1 and p_2 to indicate «world market prices». Equations [1] and [2] will still hold good, since they may be interpreted to indicate only foreign exchanges, if they are written in the form:

$$[y_1^i - x_1^i] p_1 + [y_2^i - x_2^i] p_2 = 0, \qquad i = 1, 2.$$

The expressions in parentheses represent net export surpluses.

Internal prices will now be influenced by import duties. By indicating the duties levied as a ratio between the price inclusive of duty and the price exclusive of duty and writing for this ratio τ_j^i we have:

$$\tau_j^i = \frac{p_j^i}{p_j} = \frac{p_j + t_j^i}{p_j},$$

where t_j^i represents the absolute value of the duty. Relative demand will now be different from what equations [5] and [6] indicate.

Import duties will be assumed to be levied only by country 1 on product 2 and by country 2 on product 1, since, in our numerical example, country 1 has a comparative advantage in producing product 1 and country 2 in producing product 2 [and, hence, they will have to export these products, if any]. Nevertheless, they could, of course, impose an import duty on these products if they wanted to keep their prices above world market level inside their countries; but no such price discrimination between home market and exports will be assumed here.

The relative demand equations then become, if $p_2/p_1 = \pi$:

$$\frac{x_1^1}{x_2^1} = c\,\pi\tau_2^1 + c_0 \qquad\qquad [5']$$

$$\frac{x_1^2}{x_2^2} = \frac{c\,\pi}{\tau_1^2} + c_0 \qquad\qquad [6']$$

The problems to be considered are the production and consumption patterns of both countries in the open as in well as in the closed situation, under conditions of free trade and protection. In particular, the main thesis of free trade will be proved; i.e. under free trade, the value of production at free-trade prices will be larger than under protection. It also will be shown that this is not necessarily true of the value of expenditure at free-trade prices. We will discuss our subject matter by presenting a series of precisely defined partial problems.

PROBLEM 1. *Open situation; no capacity limits; free trade.* World market prices are 1 for both products and also prevail inside both countries. Value created per hour will be equal to $1/a_j^i$ in each compartment. For country 1 it will be higher in industry 1 than in industry 2; wages will be offered up to $1/a_1^1 = 1$ and no workers can be employed in industry 2; wages, for the same reason, will be 0.5 in country 2 and no workers will be employed in industry 1. The production pattern will be:

$$\begin{bmatrix} y_1^1 & y_2^1 \\ y_1^2 & y_2^2 \end{bmatrix} = \begin{bmatrix} 10 & 0 \\ 0 & 10 \end{bmatrix}$$

and the employment pattern:

$$\begin{bmatrix} w_1^1 & w_2^1 \\ w_1^2 & w_2^2 \end{bmatrix} = \begin{bmatrix} 10 & 0 \\ 0 & 20 \end{bmatrix}$$

The value of production will amount to 10 in either country.

PROBLEM 2: *Open situation; capacity limits; free trade.* As an example, we take the capacity limits to be:

$$\begin{bmatrix} c_1^1 & c_2^1 \\ c_1^2 & c_2^2 \end{bmatrix} = \begin{bmatrix} 7 & 5 \\ 13 & 9 \end{bmatrix}$$

Consequently, no more than 7 workers can be employed in industry 1 in country 1; the other 3 will have to be engaged in industry 2; the wage level will be $1/1.1 = 0.91$. In country 2, 9 workers will be employed in industry 2; the remaining 11 will have to be engaged in industry 1 and the wage rate will be $1/2.4 = 0.42$. It appears that the capacities in the industries with a comparative advantage enter into the problem as additional bounds. The capacities in the other industries would do so only if total capacity were insufficient to employ all workers.

This problem is mainly intended to illustrate that limited capacity may act as a brake on the adaptation process from, say, a state of protection [cf. problem 3] to a state of free trade [cf. problem 1].

PROBLEM 3: *Open situation; capacity limits; protection.* Suppose that, for historical reasons [i.e. for reasons originating from the situation when transportation was much more expensive], a certain volume of production exists in the industries with comparative disadvantages. What import duties are needed to guarantee the continuation of this production? Let the capacity limits, which now have a different function from that in problem 2, be:

$$c_1^1 = \infty \qquad c_2^1 = 6$$
$$c_1^2 = 8 \qquad c_2^2 = \infty,$$

i.e. there is no limitation for c_1^1 and c_2^2. In order that 6 workers will, indeed, be attracted by industry 2 in country 1 they must be offered a wage equal to the one in industry 1, which is 1. For the employer to be able to pay this wage, he has to receive a price p_2^1 of 1.1; an import duty of 0.1 will be needed. On similar grounds, a duty of 0.2 will be needed in country 2 on product 1 [in order that its price be 1.2].

The value of production at free-trade prices will now amount to:

$$\text{Country } 1: y_1^1 + y_2^1 = w_1^1 + \frac{w_2^1}{a_2^1} = 4 + \frac{6}{1.1} = 9\frac{5}{11}.$$

$$\text{Country } 2: y_1^2 + y_2^2 = \frac{w_1^2}{a_1^2} + \frac{w_2^2}{a_2^2} = \frac{8}{2.4} + \frac{12}{2} = 9\frac{1}{3}.$$

It will be easily understood that this is, for both countries, less than the value 10 found in problem 1, as long as production is going on partly in the industries with a comparative disadvantage.

PROBLEM 4: *Closed situation; no capacity limits; free trade.* As indicated before, the demand side will now have to be brought in. The ratio of quantities demanded, evidently, depends on the numerical values of the coefficients c and c_0. It seems useful to consider the various cases that may present themselves. Depending on the relative price level, $\pi = p_2/p_1$, various production patterns may result. Each country may either produce both products or may «specialize» in one. For both products to be produced simultaneously, π has to be equal to the ratio a_2^i/a_1^i. Only product 2 will be produced if π exceeds this ratio; and only product 1 will be produced if π is below it. Since the ratio is 1.1 for country 1 and 0.83 for country 2, the following cases would appear to be possible [an asterisk indicates production and a zero no production]:

Case	Value of π	Country 1		Country 2	
		Prod. 1	Prod. 2	Prod. 1	Prod. 2
1	$\pi < 0.83$	*	o	*	o
2	$\pi = 0.83$	*	o	*	*
3	$0.83 < \pi < 1.1$	*	o	o	*
4	$\pi = 1.1$	*	*	o	*
5	$\pi > 1.1$	o	*	o	*

However, upon closer consideration it will be clear that cases 1 and 5 have to be excluded; since, in a one-commodity economy, trade does not occur.

Another conclusion following from our table is that with

$$\frac{a_2^1}{a_1^1} \neq \frac{a_2^2}{a_1^2}$$

at least one country has to specialize. Since π is not given beforehand, but follows from the equilibrium conditions expressed in equations [1]–[12], we have to solve these equations before we can know which of the cases applies. The logical structure of our problem is that c and c_0 are given and the x's, w's, y's and π are unknowns; whereas the relation between π and the w's or y's is of the discontinuous character disclosed by the above table. Mathematically, it will be simpler to assume π as given and to deduce the values for c and c_0.

Taking case 2, i.e. $w_2^1 = y_2^1 = 0$, we have, e.g., $w_1^1 = W^1 = 10$; equations [1]–[6] become:

$$10 + 0 = [0.83\, c + c_0 + 0.83]\, x_2^1$$

$$\frac{20 - w_2^2}{2.4} + \frac{w_2^2}{2} 0.83 = [0.83\, c + c_0 + 0.83]\, x_2^2$$

$$\frac{w_2^2}{2} = x_2^1 + x_2^2$$

or:

$$x_2^1 = \frac{10}{0.83(c + 1) + c_0} \qquad x_2^2 = \frac{20}{2(c + 1) + 2.4\,c_0}$$

$$w_2^2 = \frac{44}{c + 1 + 1.2\,c_0}$$

It follows that for $c + 1 + 1.2\,c_0 \gtreqless 2.2$, $w_2^2 \lesseqgtr 20$. If, therefore, $c + 1.2\,c_0 = 1.2$, the demand for commodity 2 would be so strong as to equal country 2's productive capacity, and a situation would come into existence where this country would have to specialize in product 2. The formulae would no longer be valid. Hence they hold only for:

$$c + 1.2\,c_0 \geq 1.2 \qquad\qquad [13]$$

By the same method, we find that for case 3 to apply, c and c_0 have to satisfy:

$$0.91\,[1 - c_0] < c < 1.2\,[1 - c_0] \qquad\qquad [14]$$

It will be clear that 0.91 stands for a_1^1/a_2^1 and 1.2 for a_1^2/a_2^2. It may be observed that the right-hand inequality here expressed coincides with the one implied in [13].

For case 4:

$$1.1\,c + c_0 \leq 1 \qquad\qquad [15]$$

We are now able to invert our findings, according to the logical structure of the problem, and may summarize the situation for problem 4 as follows:

$0.91\,[1 - c_0] \geq c$	$0.91\,[1 - c_0] < c <$ $1.2\,[1 - c_0]$	$c \geq 1.2\,[1 - c_0]$
$\pi = 1.1$	$1.1 > \pi > 0.83$	$\pi = 0.83$
$w_1^2 = y_1^2 = 0$	$w_1^2 = w_2^1 = y_1^2 = y_2^1 = 0$	$w_2^1 = y_2^1 = 0$
$w_2^1 = \dfrac{10 - 11\,c + 10\,c_0}{1 + c + 0.91\,c_0}$		$w_2^2 = \dfrac{44}{1 + c + 1.2\,c_0}$

121

For our further examples we choose $c_0 = 0$, $c = 1.5$, leading to:

$$\begin{bmatrix} y_1^1 & y_2^1 \\ y_1^2 & y_2^2 \end{bmatrix} = \begin{bmatrix} 10 & 0 \\ 1 & 8.8 \end{bmatrix} \; ; \begin{bmatrix} x_1^1 & x_2^1 \\ x_1^2 & x_2^2 \end{bmatrix} = \begin{bmatrix} 6 & 4.8 \\ 5 & 4 \end{bmatrix}$$

At free-trade prices, i.e. at the prices prevailing with this c_0 and c, or $\pi = 0.83$, the value of production equals, for country 1, 10 and for country 2, 8.33. These values are equal to the values of expenditure, as can be easily tested.

PROBLEM 5: *Closed situation; no capacity limits; protection.* The logical structure of this problem is very similar to that of problem 4; in addition to c_0 and c, the import duties, τ_2^1 and τ_1^2, are also given. Since they are able to change the price ratios inside the countries, there are also several possibilities as to the production pattern, depending on these data. In order not to make our argument too complicated we take the numerical values of c_0 and c chosen in problem 4, namely $c_0 = 0$, $c = 1.5$. The number of cases possible under protection is larger, since, for instance, simultaneous production of both commodities in both countries is now possible. Since the object of protection is, in many cases, to maintain such a production pattern, we will take this very case as our special numerical example. Before considering this, we should first like to give a survey of all possible cases. This may be given the following tabular form:

	$\pi \, \tau_2^1 < \dfrac{a_2^1}{a_1^1}$	$\pi \, \tau_2^1 = \dfrac{a_2^1}{a_1^1}$	$\pi \, \tau_2^1 > \dfrac{a_2^1}{a_1^1}$
$\dfrac{\pi}{\tau_1^2} < \dfrac{a_2^2}{a_1^2}$	[1] Impossible	[2] $w_2^2 = 0$	[3] $w_1^1 = w_2^2 = 0$
$\dfrac{\pi}{\tau_1^2} = \dfrac{a_2^2}{a_1^2}$	[4] $w_2^1 = 0$	[5] All $w \neq 0$	[6] $w_1^1 = 0$
$\dfrac{\pi}{\tau_1^2} > \dfrac{a_2^2}{a_1^2}$	[7] $w_1^2 = w_1^2 = 0$	[8] $w_1^2 = 0$	[9] Impossible

It appears from the table that in cases of very high duties [case [3]], even anti-specialization would be possible; in cases of low tariffs a tendency towards normal specialization [case [7]] may still exist. Cases [1] and [9] are again impossible because both countries would specialize in the same product. The case we are going to consider is case [5], for which we have the condition

$$\tau_2^1 \tau_1^2 = \frac{a_2^1}{a_1^1} \frac{a_1^2}{a_2^2}.$$

Although it may seem «improbable» that such a condition could be fulfilled by chance, it should not be overlooked that often, as has already been observed, this case is the very situation aimed at.

Mathematically, the case has the attractive feature that equations [5'] and [6'], which have now to be substituted for [5] and [6], reduce to equations without π, namely:

$$x_1^1 = 1.65 \; x_2^1$$
$$x_1^2 = 1.25 \; x_2^2$$

Furthermore, it appears that there is still a double infinity of cases fulfilling our condition; for we are left with 7 independent equations between 9 variables [4 x's, 4 y's and π]. These equations are equations [1]–[12], after eliminating, with the aid of [7]–[10], the four w's and leaving out one of the first four, [1]–[4]. The double infinity of cases evidently corresponds to the freedom which employers in both countries have, under the circumstances specified, to produce either commodity 1 or commodity 2. By every choice they make all the other variables, including π, are determined. In the case without protection such a freedom does not exist, even in the one country in which [in cases 2 and 4 of problem 4] simultaneous production in two industries occurs. For, here, any choice as to the production pattern determines not only π, the price ratio on the world market, but, at the same time, the price ratio within each country. In our present problem, where we took $\pi\tau_2^1$ and π/τ_1^2 as given, import duties are assumed to be so manipulated as to keep these internal price ratios at the values assumed.

Since we are interested only in an example, and not primarily in the complete solution of all the cases implied, we have deliberately made our choice from among the double infinity of possible solutions. This we have done, firstly, by choosing π rather than one of the y's, and, secondly, by choosing one of the y's. Our choice has been $\pi = 1$ and $y_1^2 = 2$. With regard to the latter choice, we have taken care not to choose a value – which would have been possible – leading to a negative value for one of the other y's. The following values appear to satisfy all our equations, $[1]$–$[4]$, $[5']$, $[6']$, $[7]$–$[12]$:

$$
\begin{bmatrix} y_1^1 & y_2^1 \\ y_1^2 & y_2^2 \end{bmatrix} = \begin{bmatrix} 9.52 & 0.43 \\ 2.00 & 7.60 \end{bmatrix} ; \qquad \begin{bmatrix} x_1^1 & x_2^1 \\ x_1^2 & x_2^2 \end{bmatrix} = \begin{bmatrix} 6.20 & 3.76 \\ 5.32 & 4.28 \end{bmatrix}
$$

With their help, we can now calculate the values of production and expenditure both at current world-market prices and at free-trade prices [i.e. at the prices prevailing in problem 4]. For comparison, we repeat the values found in problem 4 and summarize all results in the table below.

Value of:	At prices:	Free trade		Protection	
		Country 1	2	1	2
Production	Current	10.00	8.33	9.96	9.60
Expenditure	Current	10.00	8.33	9.96	9.60
Production	Free-trade	10.00	8.33	9.88	8.31
Expenditure	Free-trade	10.00	8.33	9.32	8.87

It appears, of course, that the values for production and expenditure in each country are equal to each other in terms of current prices, which, in the case of free trade, are, at the same time, free-trade prices. When valued on the basis of free-trade prices they are not necessarily equal in the case of protection. The differences therefore reflect the influence exerted by a change in the terms of trade as compared with free trade. In our example, country 1 suffers a loss by this change, whereas country 2 shows a gain. The value of production at free-trade prices has decreased for both countries in moving from free-trade to protection. In addition, there is evidently a decrease in the total production value for both countries together and, consequently, a lower total value of expenditure.

This applies not only to our example but would have been found to be true for any example within our model. What our example also proves is the possibility that, under protection, one country may gain on the free-trade value of its expenditure; in fact, country 2 does. This is an illustration of two important principles, namely:

[i] that the central thesis of free-trade theory cannot be proved, under the assumptions made, for any welfare concept; and

[ii] that tariffs may be used to the advantage of one country at least, to manipulate the terms of trade in such a way as to increase the free-trade value of expenditure.

Finally, it should be observed that the gain of country 2 could have been made available to that country – in the case of free trade – out of the larger gain in the total production value for the two countries together under free trade. Under free trade, total production might have been distributed between countries 1 and 2 so as to yield 8.87 to country 2 [as under protection] and leave to country 1 an amount of 9.46, which is still superior to what that country would have under protection [9.32]. This is an application of the «compensation principle» of welfare economics.

APPENDIX II – INTERNATIONAL TRADE UNDER VARIABLE RETURNS IN A VERY SIMPLE MODEL [1]

After having discussed some problems of international trade for a two-country, two-commodity model under constant returns, we will now deal with some problems under conditions of variable returns [i e. decreasing as well as increasing returns]. These problems will be concerned with the conditions under which a country will have an advantage due to international trade. Since only a comparison will be made between the situation without international trade and the situation with completely free international trade, no conclusions are drawn about any intermediary situations, e.g. situations with tariffs.

1. Measuring the «Advantage» to a Country of International Trade

Strictly speaking, it is not possible to tell whether or not a given country gains an «advantage» from the existence of international trade, since it is, on closer examination, not possible to give a precise meaning to the notion of an «advantage» to a country. It is possible to speak of an advantage to an individual person; a given change in his situation brings him either to a higher or to a lower level of satisfaction [ophelimity]. Since, for the time being, this satisfaction cannot be measured and, a fortiori, a common measure for the satisfaction of the various subjects constituting a country does not exist, it is impossible to add up the advantages or disadvantages for individual persons and, hence, to give a precise meaning to the notion of the advantage to a country. On the other hand, as a discussion of the «advantages of international trade» only makes sense if some conventional notion is accepted, we shall, in what follows, proceed as if a country as a whole also possesses a system of «indifference

---

1. This appendix forms the largest part of Appendix 1 in the first edition of this book [under the title «International Economic Co-operation»]. I have omitted the discussion with Professor Frank D. Graham since I did not arrive at different conclusions, but only doubted whether his numerical example was consistent.

curves» similar to those for an individual person. We speak only of «curves» and not of surfaces, etc., since we shall be discussing only cases in which we are dealing with two commodities, 1 and 2, the consumed quantities of which, x'_1 and x'_2, determine the «satisfaction» of the country $\Omega\ [x'_1,\ x'_2]$. Each indifference curve $\Omega\ [x'_1,\ x'_2] = C$ is composed of [is the locus of] all commodity combinations, x'_1, x'_1, that yield an equal satisfaction to a country. A combination, $x''_1,\ x''_2$, yielding a higher satisfaction than combination, $x'_1,\ x'_2$, is situated on a «higher» indifference curve, etc. We make the usual assumption that these curves turn their convex side to the origin.

2. The Possibility of Decreasing and Increasing Marginal Cost

For simplicity's sake we assume that there is only one productive agent, which we call labour. The total quantity of labour, a, is given and is fully employed. The quantities used in the production of commodities 1 and 2 are denoted by a_1 and a_2; hence

$$a_1 + a_2 = a \qquad\qquad [1]$$

The quantity a_1 depends on the quantity x_1 of commodity 1 it is desired to produce; likewise, a_2 depends on x_2:

$$a_1 = \varphi_1\ [x_1] \qquad\qquad [2]$$

$$a_2 = \varphi_2\ [x_2] \qquad\qquad [3]$$

The functions φ_1 and φ_2 are called *cost functions*. Marginal cost in each case is $\varphi'_1\ [x_1]$ and $\varphi'_2\ [x_2]$, respectively; these expressions always have positive values. They may, however, be increasing or decreasing functions of x_1 and x_2. The case of *increasing marginal cost* is the normal case. *Decreasing marginal cost* for a whole branch of industry will hardly occur. Even if the «law of decreasing marginal cost» is assumed to prevail for a single enterprise, it need not be valid for the industry as a whole. The law will, as a rule, only exist for certain ranges of the quantity produced in a single enterprise. It is a well-known fact that no situation of competitive equilibrium is possible within such a range. If the industry is composed of more than one enterprise, an extension of production will imply the necessity of bringing into use less productive firms, i.e. increasing marginal cost. Only if the most economic size of the unit exceeds the size of the branch as a whole will there be one enterprise; in this case, competitive equilibrium within the range of decreasing marginal cost is also not possible.

3. *A Graphical Representation of the Equilibrium of Production and International Trade*

In fig. 1 let x_1 and x_1' be measured along the positive part of the horizontal axis and x_2 and x_2' along the positive part of the vertical axis. The negative halves of these axes are used for plotting a_1 and

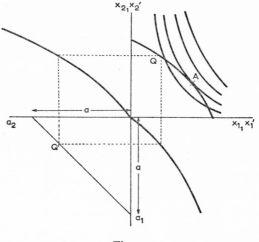

Fig. 1.

a_2, respectively. In the fourth quadrant we draw the cost curve $a_1 = \varphi_1[x_1]$, assumed to be of the normal [convex] type. In the second quadrant the curve $a_2 = \varphi_2[x_2]$ is drawn in a similar way; to begin with, it is also assumed to be convex in an upward direction. In the third quadrant the line $a_1 + a_2 = a$ is indicated, being the locus of all possible applications of productive resources. From these data the «*production curve*» may be deduced, indicating all combinations, x_1, x_2, that the country is able to produce. This curve has the equation:

$$\varphi_1[x_1] + \varphi_2[x_2] = a \tag{4}$$

Any point Q of this curve is obtained from the corresponding point

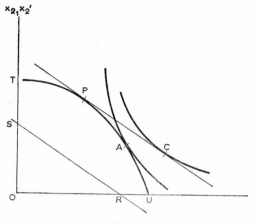

Fig. 2.

Q' of the line [1] given by the dotted lines in fig. 1. In the absence of international trade, the quantities produced, x_1 and x_2, coincide with the quantities consumed, x_1' and x_2'. For its consumption the country has, therefore, to choose between the points on the production curve only. It will attain maximum satisfaction if it chooses point A where the production curve is tangent to one of the ophelimity curves plotted against the x_1 - x_2-axes; there is no point with a higher satisfaction to be found on the production curve. Under free competition this point will be attained automatically. The price relation between commodities 1 and 2 will be indicated by the absolute value of the slope of the common tangent line to the two curves at A; i.e. this slope indicates the ratio between the quantity of x_2 exchanged for a unit of x_1; i.e. the price of x_1 in terms of x_2.

Now, let us assume that an opportunity is offered of buying or selling in an international market at a given price p [of x_1 in terms of x_2] represented graphically by the slope of the line R S in fig. 2 [where the first quadrant of fig. 1 has been reproduced]. This means that x_1 no longer has to coincide with x_1' nor x_2 with x_2'.

A «consumption point», x_1', x_2', may now be reached which is different from the «production point», x_1, x_2, and connected to the latter by the equation:

$$x_1' = x_1 + \frac{1}{p}[x_2 - x_2']$$ [5]

indicating that the consumption of commodity 1 equals its production, x_1, plus the quantity bought in the international market, at a price p, for a quantity $x_2 - x_2'$, of commodity 2. The consumption of 2 is now less than x_2. Of course, x_2' may also be $> x_2$, but then x_1' will be $< x_1$.

Fig. 2 clearly discloses what the new equilibrium situation will be. With the given price ratio, p, producers will find it advantageous to use their productive resources in another way than before. In the case assumed in fig. 2, where p is lower than the price ratio prevailing at point A, it will pay them to produce more of commodity 2 and less of commodity 1; equilibrium will be attained only if the marginal products obtained are of equal value. This means that they will proceed to point P, where the tangent line to the production curve is parallel to the given line RS. Having produced the quantities, x_1, x_2, corresponding to P, the country is now free to exchange part of its production at the terms expressed in equation [5]; i.e., in graphical language, it is free to move along the «price line» PC. It will do so until it has reached the point of maximum satisfaction, which is point C, where P is tangent to an indifference curve. The new equilibrium is, therefore, represented by the two points, P, C, the «*production*» and the «*consumption points*», respectively.

Under conditions later to be enumerated, the *satisfaction obtained in the new situation will always be greater than that obtained in the old one*. For P C, as a tangent to a convex curve, will, for any value of x_1, show a higher value of x_2 than the corresponding point of the production curve[1]. Since the equilibrium point in the absence of international trade, A, is necessarily a point of the production curve, the satisfaction at C always exceeds that at A, except in the particular case where A and C coincide, i.e. where the price ratio p on the world market equals the price ratio existing without international trade. Hence, under the conditions to be discussed, *the introduction of international trade always means an advantage* to a country; with the

1. From P to the left, $\dfrac{dx_2}{dx_1}$ for the production curve is, in absolute measure, always smaller than $\left|\dfrac{dx_2}{dx_1}\right|$ for the price line; from P to the right $\left|\dfrac{dx_2}{dx_1}\right|$ for the production curve is always larger than $\left|\dfrac{dx_2}{dx_1}\right|$ for the price line.

exception of such border-line cases where the advantage is zero.

4. *Non-Tangent Price Line*

This important conclusion has been reached on the assumption of a number of conditions, the influence of which we will investigate in the following sections. The conditions are that:
[i]   the production curve is convex in an upward direction,
[ii] prices are equal to marginal costs,
[iii] there exists a point P on the production curve where the slope of the tangent equals the price ratio p on the world market.
First, we shall eliminate the last condition. It is, in fact, conceivable, that the price prevailing on the world market will be lower or higher than the absolute value of the slope of any tangent to the production curve. In the case of a convex curve this only means that it is lower than the slope for T or higher than that for U, the two terminal points of the production curve. In those cases, the production point will coincide with T or U, respectively; the conclusions drawn remain valid, however, as is clearly seen from the diagram.

5. *Concave Production Curve*

Next, we eliminate the first condition mentioned in section 4. This condition is closely associated with the nature of the cost curves assumed. If both cost curves are of the increasing marginal cost type, the production curve is convex. It may also be convex, however, if one of the cost curves is of another type. This depends on the degree to which the cost curve deviates from the normal type. We shall go into this question in section 6 below. Now, we start from the other end and we assume that both cost curves reflect decreasing marginal cost curves. Graphically, this means that both these curves are themselves concave and it easily follows that the production curve will also be concave upward [fig. 3]. Now all points on the production curve, except the terminal points, are *unstable equilibria*. Extension of the production of one of the commodities at the expense of the other always means an increase in total value of production; the expanding industry becomes more productive and the declining industry less productive than at the initial point.

131

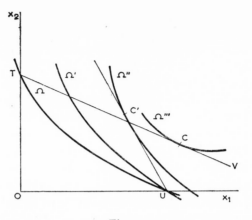

Fig. 3.

If an opportunity for international trade is created at a price ratio corresponding to the slope of a line TV, point T will be the more advantageous point and, in line with our discussion above [section 3], a consumption point C will be chosen. Generally, point T will, in the presence of trading opportunities, be the production point if the price of 1 in terms of 2 is lower than the figure corresponding to the line TU, whereas U will be the production point if the price is higher than that figure. As an example of this latter situation, the price line UC' is drawn, with a consumption point C'.

Again, the conclusion can be drawn that the *introduction of international trade increases the satisfaction to be obtained for the country*, with the exception of possible [but not necessarily existing] border-line cases. One border-line case is the one where the price line through U coincides with the tangent to the ophelimity curve through that point [Ω'].

6. *A Straight Line as Production Curve; Mixed Cases*

As a special case, often made use of in simple expositions of the theory of international trade [cf. appendix 1], we now consider the case where the cost curves are straight lines, the case of *constant marginal costs*. The production curve is now a straight line, too, each point of which is a point of indifferent equilibrium. Apart from this difference from the preceding case, the same conclusions are valid.

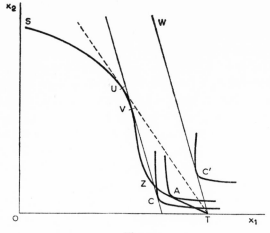

Fig. 4.

More complications arise if one of the industries operates under increasing and the other under decreasing marginal costs. Whether the production curve is convex, concave or of a more complicated type depends therefore on the exact form of the two cost curves. If one cost curve is «highly» convex and the other only «slightly» concave, the production curve will be convex, etc. There may be ranges where convexity – and others where concavity – prevails.

In order to maintain that, also in these cases of a «mixed» production curve, our statement about the advantage of international trade holds true, we will consider an arbitrary case of this type [cf. fig. 4].

For prices lower than the slope of TU a stable production equilibrium will be found between U and S. The consumption point will be either on the outside of the production curve or, in border-line cases, on the curve itself. Therefore, the satisfaction will be at least as great as before the existence of international trade.

For prices higher than the slope of TU – for example T W – point T will be one possible production point. The corresponding consumption point will lie on TW – such as C' – and hence – apart from border-line cases – will have a higher satisfaction level than in the absence of international trade.

This is not, however, the whole story. For some prices in this range there are two equilibrium points. At a price only slightly higher than that corresponding to TU – say TW – there is a possible production point in the neighbourhood of U, such as V, since the production curve is also convex for some distance below U. The corresponding consumption point will be C, yielding a lower satisfaction than without trade [point A]. The existence of two equilibrium points is nothing new; it has been discussed in some detail by Koopmans[1]. It implies that, if, by trial and error over small distances of the production curve, one of these equilibrium points is found and persists, the possibility exists that this point is not the absolute optimum but only a relative one. If we assume complete knowledge of all data on the part of the economic subjects, they will finally choose the absolute optimum.

If that knowledge is not assumed to exist, they may stay at the lower, relative, maximum. In that latter case it may happen that the consumption point is one of lower satisfaction than the one prevailing before international trade was introduced. This case occurs if the course of the ophelimity curves happens to be such that the tangent point lies below Z [cf. fig. 4]. It then lies within the production curve.

Hence, one condition has to be maintained in these mixed cases: perfect market knowledge.

7. Calculation of Prices on the Basis of Average instead of Marginal Cost

Finally, we have to investigate the consequence of the elimination of condition [ii] [section 4]. This appears to be a more serious threat to the validity of our statement. The necessity of assuming that prices are not equal to marginal costs of production only exists in the case of a decreasing marginal costs function. In industries where this is the rule, the equality of prices and marginal cost would entail a permanent loss to the producers. Hence, it is probable that, in the long run, prices will be higher than the marginal cost and, in fact, equal to average cost. In order to study the consequences of this hypothesis, let us assume that industry 1 operates at decreasing marginal cost and that production is adjusted to its price in such a way as to make average cost equal to price. Since average costs are higher than marginal cost, this means

1. J. G. KOOPMANS, «De mogelijkheid van meervoudig economisch evenwicht», *De Economist*, 81 [1932], pp. 679, 766 and 841, and «Marginale kosten, marginale opbrengsten en optimale productie-omvang» in *Economische opstellen aangeboden aan Prof. Mr. F. de Vries*, Haarlem, 1944, p. 149.

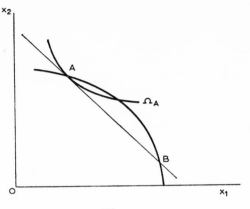

Fig. 5.

that the [absolute value of the] slope of the price line is now, at the equilibrium point, higher than the slope of the tangent.

Let us further assume that the production curve is still convex. For the equilibrium point without international trade a point A will now be chosen, where the tangents to the production curve and the ophelimity curve are no longer identical. The price line AB now intersects the production curve, since its slope must be higher than that of the tangent. It is still a tangent to the ophelimity curve. This means that the point of maximum satisfaction on the production line is no longer chosen; this method of calculating prices is disadvantageous to the particular country [cf. fig. 5].

Now consider the case with international trade [fig. 6]. Let PQ be the price line and P the corresponding production point. There are now two possibilities, indicated in fig. 6 by the subscripts 1 and 2 and by continuous and dotted ophelimity curves, respectively. In the first case, where the ophelimity curve through A, Ω_{A1} does not intersect PQ, the consumption point C_1 shows, in fact, a lower degree of satisfaction than A. Here, *international trade is a disadvantage to the particular country*. In the second case, where the ophelimity curve through A, Ω_{A2} does intersect PQ, the satisfaction at C_2 is again higher than that at A, and our former statement remains valid. Since both possibilities must be recognized, it follows that the elimination of condition [ii] [section 4] is vital to our statement. Hence, our general conclusions may be reformulated as follows: *in the simple case considered [two*

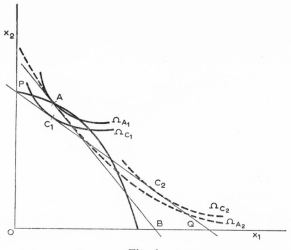

Fig. 6.

commodities and one agent of production] international trade constitutes an advantage [or as a border-line case no disadvantage] to every country involved, provided that:

1. *there is perfect knowledge of market data and*
2. *prices are calculated on the basis of marginal cost.*

8. *A Diagram for Two Countries*

So far, we have only considered the position of one country vis-à-vis a world market with a *given price ratio p* for commodity 1 in terms of commodity 2. We shall now try to answer the question as to *how that ratio* is itself determined in the simplified case where there is only one other country in that «world» market. The answer may be supplied by a simple extension of our graphical method. In fig. 7, relating, as far as our first country, «country A», is concerned, to the same situation as fig. 2, the co-ordinates x_1, x_2, x_1' and x_2' are, as before, plotted from the origin O. The corresponding co-ordinates for country B, denoted by y_1, y_2, y_1' and y_2', are plotted from O', but in the opposite direction. The point O' is simply chosen in such a way that its co-ordinates with respect to O are $x_1 + y_1$ and $x_2 + y_2$, respectively, or, which is the same, $x_1' + y_2'$ and $x_1' + y_2'$. This implies that A's and B's production points coincide at point P and their consumption points coincide

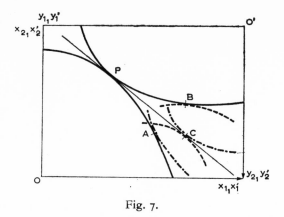

Fig. 7.

at point C. A's ophelimity curves are indicated by a line of dots and dashes, whereas B's are indicated by dashes. The points A and B are the production [and consumption] points of countries A and B, respectively, in the absence of international trade. The essence of the graphical representation is that PC is, at the same time, tangent to both production curves in P and to an ophelimity curve of each country in C. For the case represented, that of convex production curves and point P for neither country in a «border-line situation», the advantage of international trade to both countries is clear; the satisfaction to A is greater at C than at A and the satisfaction to B is greater at C than at B. The diagram cannot be constructed unless the position of C is given and this depends on the unknowns of the problem, namely x_1, x_2, y_1 and y_2. Hence, it might seem that the diagram is of no help for finding p. As a matter of fact, all these unknowns must be determined simultaneously, i.e. we must experiment with O', until a position is found where there exists – which is not generally the case – a common double tangent line to the system of ophelimity curves and the two production curves.

There are a great number of different possibilities with regard to the shape of the production curves and the situation of the production and consumption points, including quite a number of border-line cases. It can be left to the reader to go into these questions.

INDEX

Monetary Fund, International, 85, 89, 101, 104
Multilateralism, 16, 22, 42
Multiple exchange rates, 33, 49

Net position, 18
Network of flows, 16
Neutral instruments, 60

Objectives of economic policy, 62
Open flows, 16
Optimum centralization, 21, 96
Optimum policy, 26, 57
Optimum population, 9
Optimum speed of integration, 77
Optimum tariff, 25
Organization for Economic Co-operation and Development (Organization for European Economic Co-operation), 21, 88, 99, 102, 104

Parity, 36, 39
Partial customs union *cum* investment plan, 94
Payments Union, European, 88
Planning, supra-national, 79
Point Four, U.S., 103
Policy, economic, 57, 62
Population, 5, 6
Population problem, 91, 105
PÖYHÖNEN, P., 14
Price policy, 71, 86
Product, national, 6
Production, factors of, 5
PULLIAINEN, K., 14

Qualitative policy, 57
Quantitative policy, 57
Quantitative restrictions, 19, 74
Quotas, 19

Raw material markets, 100
Raw material standard, 40
Redistribution of incomes, 79
Regional integration, 98
Reserve, 40, 85, 86, 89
Resources, full use of, 26
Rome, Treaty of, 76, 77, 88, 99

SARGENT, J. R., 44

SAUNDERS, C., 31
Schuman Plan, 105
Soft currencies, 42
Special Fund of U.N., 103
Spending equilibrium, 48, 102
Sterling area, 43, 44, 46
Sterling balances, 87, 89
STERN, R. M., 22
Subsidies, 74, 78, 79
Supporting instruments, 60, 68
Supra-national authority, 67
Supra-national planning, 79

Targets of economic policy, 62
Tariff, common, 21
Tariff, optimum, 25
Tariff reduction, 80, 99
Tax policy, 70, 74
Taxes, indirect, 68, 78
Technical Assistance Board, 104
Terms of trade, 55
TINBERGEN, J., 14, 58
Trade flows, 19
Trade Organization, International, 99
Trade restrictions, 99
Trade-creating elements, 28
Trade-diverting elements, 28
Transfer, 33
Transfer of knowledge, 104
Transferability of sterling, 44
Treasury, international, 103
Treaty of Rome, 76, 77, 88, 99
TRIFFIN, ROBERT, 85, 102

Unilateral payments, 35
Uniformity, 68
Union, economic, 21
Union, customs, 21, 28, 94, 99
Unit, International, 7
United Nations, 98, 101
U.N. Committee for International Commodity Trade, 100
U.N. Economic and Social Council, 94, 102
U.N. Educational, Scientific and Cultural Organization, 104
U.N. General Assembly, 93, 94
U.N. Secretariat, 79, 94, 104
U.N. Special Fund, 103
U.S. Point Four, 103

PRINTED IN THE NETHERLANDS